A Better Yesterday

Living Life After Abuse

D0109706

A Better Yesterday
Living Life After Abuse

Roger Dean Kiser

Health Communications, Inc.
Deerfield Beach, Florida

www.hcibooks.com

Some names have been changed to protect the privacy of certain individuals.

Library of Congress Cataloging-in-Publication Data
Kiser, Roger Dean.
  A better yesterday : living life after abuse / Roger Dean Kiser.
      p. cm.
    ISBN-13: 978-0-7573-1360-8
    ISBN-10: 0-7573-1360-4
    1. Kiser, Roger Dean.   2. Abused children—United States—
  Biography.   3. Adult child abuse victims—United States—
  Biography.   I. Title.
  HV6626.52.K57A3 2010
  362.76092—dc22
  [B]

2009048642

Publisher: Health Communications, Inc.
              3201 S.W. 15th Street
              Deerfield Beach, FL 33442-8190

Cover design by Larissa Hise Henoch
Interior design by Lawna Patterson Oldfield
Interior formatting by Dawn Von Strolley Grove

Contents

Introduction

Most people who were or are abused are always looking to the future, a better tomorrow, in the hope of finding happiness. A new experience, a new car, winning the lottery, or falling in love always seems to ease the pain and sadness, at least for a short period. At age fifty-two, I came to the realization that the future did not hold the answers I sought. Most of my future had already passed me by, and I had very little time left to try to find some form of happiness. It was then that I began to search my past for any answers that might be hidden, and it was in that past that I finally found the happiness and the comfort I had always sought.

Despite the years of verbal, physical, emotional, and sexual abuse I suffered as a child, one evening I decided to sit down and try to make a list of the few positive things (if there were any) that happened during my childhood and as a young man. I was rather surprised when right before my eyes the list began to grow. Within days, the positive list far outweighed the negative list. I then began to wonder, *If the positive list is fifty times longer than the negative list, why does the negative list hold so much power over me?*

For days I pondered that thought.

While mowing the lawn early one evening, I began thinking about a painful incident that had happened to me on my first day at a new high school. As usual, the boys were inspecting the girls and the girls were inspecting the boys. While I was walking down the hallway, there were as many as ten girls who winked, batted their eyelashes, or smiled at me. I heard a couple of them whisper, "He's cute," or "He's nice-looking."

Just as I was about to enter my mechanical drawing class, a beautiful girl near the doorway looked at me, snickered, and said to her girlfriend, "Jesus Christ, look at that big nose he's got." My face grew hot. I was devastated and almost did not enter the classroom. I wanted to run away, never to be seen or heard from again. I went to class, but the girl's words haunted me—up until this moment, nearly forty years later.

I stopped mowing and stood there thinking, *How can what one girl said far outweigh what ten other girls had said minutes earlier?* It was then and there that I began to realize the answer to my problem. I clearly saw that I had chosen to live my entire life based on a few falsehoods rather than on the truth.

With my life now more than half over, I had to quickly decide: What is the truth?

Many adults who were abused as children have allowed a few irresponsible individuals from their past to destroy their future happiness—all thanks to nothing more than a handful of lies and distorted self-interest. I too had allowed the lies and the abuse I suffered at the hands of my caretakers to define my past, but now I choose to focus on the comfort and the happiness that I also experienced throughout my life, which helped to shape me into the caring person I am today. In this book, I share those stories—about the kind people, the loving animals, and the positive events that were comforting lights in a dark tunnel. Without them, I would have never found my way out.

In this book, I share with you some of the experiences that most affected my life for the good. Although the stories appear mostly in chronological order, to the best of my memory, they span many years. You may wish to know exact dates and more details, but this is not the story of my life. Rather, these stories are snapshots from my life. The *where, when,* and *what happened next* are not the focus. What I write about and share with you are my memories of the kindness and the respect that I received from special people and animals over the years, as well as several events I witnessed that touched my heart or taught me a valuable lesson about life. Many of these experiences transformed some of the hatred that was lurking in my heart into warm and wonderful feelings.

I didn't recognize these feelings as a young child in an abusive orphanage or later as a teenager in a horrific institution for wayward boys. Nevertheless, the feelings and emotions were there and, fortunately, remained with me my entire life, just waiting for recognition and attention. Because of these positive experiences, I was able to return these special feelings to others during the course of my life. It is those feelings, and those feelings alone, that allowed me to learn about the kindness of the human spirit and taught me to love my children, my grandchildren, and my fellow human beings.

The wooden church doors opened, and everyone turned to look at the latecomer. He lowered his head and kept his eyes on the tile floor as he walked slowly toward the far back pew, away from the rest of the congregation. He was thin, dirty, and unshaven. He had no shoes.

The preacher immediately stopped talking and lowered his arms, which he had been flinging about during his sermon. He turned his gaze toward the man, who shifted the heavy wooden bench as he took his seat. The deacons and the choirmaster whispered among themselves while several other members of the church turned to gawk at the unshaven figure.

The man smiled at us—the little children from the orphanage—whenever we would turn around to look at him, which we did often and couldn't help doing. The matron reached over and slapped me on the leg when I dropped my nickel for the collection plate onto our wooden bench, so I tried to sit very still and not turn around anymore. Nevertheless, I managed to sneak a few peeks without her noticing.

The preacher started talking again, but now he was going on and on about how people should dress up for church and that they should cut their hair and be clean before coming to services. I knew that he was saying what he was saying to make the man in the back of the church feel bad. The man didn't seem to mind; he just sat there quietly, smiling.

As the sermon progressed, however, the man raised his hands toward the ceiling and said in a deep voice, "Praise the Father in heaven!"

Now everyone turned around, including the matron. The church people looked at him as though he were crazy, but I didn't think he was crazy. The preacher finally walked away from the altar and whispered something to the deacon. The deacon got up from his chair and walked down the side isle next to the stained-glass windows. In hushed tones, he asked the man to leave. The man looked up at the deacon and smiled. Without saying a word, he rose to his feet, turned, and walked toward the exit.

As he reached the wooden doors, he stopped, turned around, and smiled. He reached over and picked up the stack of religious literature that sat on the table by the doors. He turned them facedown, then he pulled open the large wooden doors and left.

I will never forget what I saw in that man's smile: kindness. Yet he was asked to leave the church that Sunday morning simply because of how he looked and for praising the Lord—out loud. However, he sure looked an awful lot like the man in the glossy pictures in the middle of the Bible I was holding in my hands.

"Am I a Children?"

I was very excited and smiling from ear to ear. It was several days before Christmas, and all the children from the orphanage had been bused to a hotel in downtown Jacksonville, Florida, to attend a Christmas party for underprivileged kids.

We stood behind our assigned seats until the man on the stage said a prayer. Then he told everyone to sit down. Within minutes, we were served a meal that seemed to me to be fit for a king. We received our meals on real dishes, which were filled with large pieces of meat and many green vegetables. There were two big puffy rolls with real butter on a small dish beside each plate. I ate until I could eat no more. I remember thinking how nice it would be to eat that kind of food every day. How wonderful it would be to go to bed at night without my stomach aching.

As we ate, some people performed a Christmas play up on the large stage. Suddenly the lights dimmed, and everyone became quiet. When the lights were turned back on, Santa Claus came walking out onto the stage. The kids went wild with excitement. They began clapping their hands and yelling as loud as they could.

I too was excited, but I knew better than to yell or to jump up and scream. Mrs. Winters, the head matron, sat only three seats away from me. She made it very clear to us all that we were to conduct ourselves in "a proper manner" and that there was to be "no yelling or screaming." Therefore, I just sat with my hands underneath my legs. However, I really wanted to yell out, 'cause I was really happy inside.

One orphan at a time was led up onto the stage, and Santa Claus handed each child a gift.

Please let me get a large gift, I kept thinking.

The line became shorter and shorter, and my turn finally came. Santa looked at me, smiled, and then winked. He reached over and handed me a large box with two gold ribbons on it. As I leaned forward to take the box, I tripped and fell to my knees. Santa reached over and helped me to my feet.

"Move it along, Kiser," scolded Mother Winters.

I was now leaning against Santa Claus's leg and looking directly into his eyes. His face was less than an inch from mine.

"Can I hug you, Santa?" I asked.

The next thing I knew, Mother Winters snatched me up by my shirt collar and pulled me away.

Santa stood up, raised his hand into the air, and shouted, "Ma'am, please! These are children!"

Mother Winters never even looked back; she just kept on walking and pushing me down the stage stairs and back into the dining area. I sat down in my chair, crying. Occasionally, I looked up at the stage to see if my gift was still sitting by Santa Claus.

When the party was over, Mother Winters hurried us back to our buses. We all lined up, waiting to board. All the kids were going on about their gifts from Santa, but I didn't have one.

"Ho, ho, ho," I heard behind me.

My heart jumped. I turned around, and there stood Santa Claus holding my box. He set it down on the ground beside me.

"You forgot this," he said. Then he knelt down and hugged me as hard as he could.

"Am I a children?" I whispered.

"You're a good children," he said, as he let go of me.

When I looked up into his face, I saw something that no one else in the world has ever seen. I saw that Santa himself had a tear in his eye.

Christmastime in the City

The sidewalks were decorated in holiday style as an old familiar song played from the large speakers that hung outside the front door of the department store. I twirled around, looking in awe at all the beautiful lights that lined the downtown streets of Jacksonville. Even the taillights of the cars looked festive as they passed us by.

Silver bells, silver bells, it's Christmastime in the city.

When I stopped twirling, I caught my reflection in the large plate-glass window of a store. I reached out and touched my face in the window. I was excited, but my reflection looked sad. "I got two dollars to spend. I can be happy now," I told myself quietly, but it didn't work. I wasn't happy.

Soon it will be Christmas Day.

I leaned against the plate-glass window and began to cry.

"What's wrong?" asked one of the chaperones from

the men's club that sponsored our trip. He knelt down and put his arm around my shoulder.

"I never seen myself look unhappy in the Christmas lights before," I answered honestly.

"Why do you suppose you are so unhappy?" the man asked, and I felt his arm tighten around my shoulder.

"The orphanage," I said, as if that explained everything.

"Oh, it can't be that bad. Can it?" he asked.

"It's bad. It's really, really bad. Just this morning, the matron called me ugly."

Suddenly I began crying again.

"How old are you?" the man asked.

"I just turned seven a while ago," I told him through my tears, then asked, "Do you think someday a girl will think that I'm pretty, even with these here big ears?"

"You are a very handsome little boy," he replied with a smile.

"Does handsome make me pretty?" I asked.

The man laughed and said, "All children are pretty."

I looked up into his smiling face, and all my sadness seemed to melt away.

"You remember that, okay?" he told me.

I nodded. No one could smile like that and be telling a lie.

He stood up and said to the group, "Let's take you boys to the movies!"

I joined the other boys, and we headed to the theatre. The man bought us all the popcorn and candy we wanted. I thought how wonderful it was that someone who didn't even know us would spend his own money on kids like us. We all laughed at the funny movie and had a good time. Each time the man would laugh hard, he'd pat me on top of the head and rustle my hair. I looked up at him each time, and he would just keep smiling his great big wonderful smile.

I can still close my eyes and remember his kindness. When costly gifts are long gone and buried away in some distant landfill, that sort of gift—the gift that costs nothing—lives on to be shared with others. Kindness is a present that will never be tossed aside.

Honey

One day, while I was playing in the dirt pile behind the boys' dormitory at the orphanage, I heard a strange noise behind me. I jumped up and spun around quickly, afraid that I was in trouble with the matron, as usual. When I stood up, I saw the most beautiful, kind, and loving face looking at me.

The eyes of an angel gazed only at me! My heart skipped a beat for the first time in my young life. I placed my hands on my cheeks and took a deep breath. With wide eyes and an open mouth, I backed up slowly against the oak tree and waited to see what would happen next. She just stood there like a statue and did not say anything at all.

I looked her up and down, from head to toe. I noticed the beautiful brown and white coat she wore. After a minute or so, I slowly reached out and touched it. She opened her mouth but then closed it again without making a sound. I quickly withdrew my hand, because I did not want to get in trouble. Then I placed it behind me to show her that I was sorry for touching her and that I wouldn't do it again. Still she said nothing. I sat back down in the dirt pile and kept my eyes on my task.

Finally, she came closer and touched me gently on the face. She was warm, and it felt good to be touched by someone or something that did not want to hurt me. I kept looking down, because I did not want to look her directly in the eyes. At the orphanage, looking someone in the eyes was discouraged because it was considered confrontational, so I knew better.

Then I could take it no longer. It seemed safe, so I reached out with both hands and put them around her. When she licked my face, I knew she liked me, too.

I had no idea where she came from. We had never had a dog at the orphanage (and never would again). Later that day, we boys named the big old bird dog Honey. We loved her, and she loved all of us. It was absolutely wonderful.

About two weeks later, one of the boys came running to my room. Sobbing, he told me that Honey had been run over by a car outside the orphanage gate. I ran downstairs as fast as I could and locked myself in the telephone room. Then I stood there against the locked door, breathing in and out as fast as I could. I could not come out, not even for supper; I stayed there and cried all night long.

The next day I could not even go out the front gate for fear of seeing Honey lying dead in the road, so I climbed over the orphanage fence to go to school. After school, the head matron called me to the office and told me to go with old Mack, the groundskeeper, to get a wheelbarrow and pick Honey up out of the road. I will never forget that sight as long as I live; it was worse than horrible. Her insides were all over the place.

I will always remember the look on Honey's face as she lay there dead with her tongue hanging out. I knew that this beautiful old dog would never love me again. I stood there and cried the entire time as I tried not to smell the odor of death. Mack, who was a very kind old man, told me not to look at her. All by himself, he moved her into the wheelbarrow and picked up all the pieces. Then he took her away to bury her. I do not know where he buried her, and I did not want to know.

There was never anyone to hold us or to tell us that everything was going to be all right. Day after day, our little hearts were ripped to pieces, and there was no one who cared. All that the matron saw was a dead dog lying in the middle of the road and "a bunch of whining, crying little animals."

Poor old Honey was just another thing that got in her way—just as we did.

Old Mack came shuffling back with his shovel, his jaw working the way it did when he was thinking.

"Honey was a good dog," he said.

Somehow Mack understood that Honey had given me a taste of what love feels like. "Shame no one's watching out for helpless creatures," he added.

It might have been just then and there that I decided to protect helpless animals any way I could. Although it would be many years before I could really make a difference, Honey's love was never forgotten.

The Most Beautiful Voice I Ever Heard

"Would you be kind enough to read something for me?" asked the old hobo as we tried to stay out of sight beneath the overpass. Having run away from the orphanage again, I found solace beneath the railroad overpass for a few days. I knew that this was a good place to come, because word at the orphanage had it that an abundance of food could always be found under the overpass with its never-ending flow of hobos.

I nodded my head and watched as the old man rummaged through the dirty brown gunnysack slung over his shoulder.

He removed various items from the sack, then shouted, "Here it is, sonny!"

He held up the item in his shaking hands.

"What is that thing?" I asked. "I ain't never seen no kind of paper card thing like that before. Hey, it's got a stamp on it. It is like a letter?"

"It's called a postcard."

I reached out, took the dirty wrinkled postcard from his hand, and carefully looked at both sides. Taking my time, I inspected every inch of this strange new item. The date was stamped on the back, covering part of the writing.

"Can you please read that to me?" he requested again.

"You're kinda old, mister, don't you know how to read nothin'?" I asked.

"My eyes don't work like they used to," he explained, squinting.

Raising the card, I began to read the large print: "Carl, glad you made it to America. I know you will be a success in such a wonderful place. Love, Mini."

"Who's Mini?" I asked the man.

"She's my sister. She lives in Paris."

"I know where that is. It's over the ocean."

As he shook his head back and forth, tears slowly rolled down the old man's dirty cheeks.

"Thank you for the beans, mister. It sure was good of you to share," I said, as I held the postcard out to him.

Reaching out, he took the card and stuffed it into the pocket of his torn wool overshirt. Then, without saying a word, he walked back over to the large fire barrel and began to warm his hands.

The orphanage matrons had always told me that I

was "not the brightest bulb on the tree." Even considering that, I knew when someone wanted or did not want to talk. Keeping my mouth shut, I walked over to the rusty fifty-five-gallon drum and stood there, not speaking.

Several minutes later, the old man began to sing. He had one of the most beautiful voices I had ever heard. I had listened to many people sing on the little black-and-white Zenith television at the orphanage, but nothing I had ever heard was as beautiful as the voice coming from the old man.

Hearing something behind me, I turned around and saw two railroad guards, blackjacks in hand, heading toward us. All of a sudden they stopped to listen to the singing. I could tell that they too were amazed by such a wonderful and joyous sound.

I stood waiting for the two men to begin beating the two of us for hiding beneath the overpass. For almost a minute or two the two guards did not move a muscle. Then one of the men tapped his blackjack on the stomach of the other guard and motioned with his head, in a backward direction. The two of them turned and began walking away, back toward the railroad yard.

When the old man stopped singing, I looked over

at him and said, "You really need to be on television, mister. Really, you do."

"I'll never sing to the public again," he replied.

"Why not?"

"I was forced to sing for the Germans during the war. No, I'll never sing for others again—just for you, little boy, for reading to me. Thank you."

Once again, tears began to roll down the old man's cheeks. Throwing his gunnysack over his shoulder, he began walking down the railroad tracks.

For several minutes, I stood watching the old man with the most beautiful voice disappear into the distance. Despite his sadness, his voice had filled my heart.

Brains and Brawn

Finally, we were on our way to recess. Our teacher, Mrs. Cherry, had just finished giving us a speech—maybe it was a lesson—about brains and brawn, so we were itching to get outside and get moving again. The recess teacher said to line up to pick teams for dodgeball.

Kids from the orphanage were always the last to be picked for a team for any type of a game at school: baseball, football, and even dodgeball. It didn't seem to make a difference if we were tall or short, thin or fat, or fast or slow. The fact that we came from the orphanage seemed to be all that mattered to those who did the choosing.

One day, I was chosen to be one of the captains for a game of dodgeball. I was pleasantly surprised, because even the teachers usually treated us as though we were different from the kids with homes. My team was going to be the best—I knew who was the fastest and who had the best aim. This was the day I was going to be a winner!

We gathered in a group on the playground, and the teacher flipped a coin to see which captain would be the first to pick.

When the coin landed, our teacher called out, "Heads!"

I smiled widely—I was the one who'd picked heads.

I scanned the group, and my eyes stopped at Jeffrey. He was slow and heavy and was always picked last. I am not sure what came over me, but at that moment, winning the game did not seem so important to me.

"Jeffrey!" I yelled, pointing to him.

He looked up in total shock, then began moving his massiveness toward me.

"You picked me?" he asked.

I reached over and patted him on the back.

My next pick was Leonard. He was a small boy who wore black thick-rimmed glasses and never combed his hair. He was the quiet type and was not liked by very many of the popular kids. He was without a doubt the brain of the class. The remainder of my picks were kids I knew from the orphanage or kids who were always the last to be picked.

"He picked a bunch of losers," said the captain of the other team. "We're gonna win without even trying."

"We're gonna lose," said Jeffrey, as our team huddled in a tight circle.

"Of course we're gonna lose," I told them.

"Then why did you pick me?" asked Jeffrey.

"And why did you pick me?" Leonard echoed. "I can't see without my glasses."

As the game started, I made sure that Jeffrey stood behind those of us who were faster. That way, he could get out of the way of the ball before it reached him. I made sure that my team did not stay in the center of the circle. We moved around the circle rather than across it. That seemed to give us a big advantage.

The ball was thrown five or six times before one of my teammates was hit, and another five or six times before another was knocked out. One at a time, my team members were hit and fell out. The other team hit us with the ball as hard as possible, slamming the ball against our backs when we could not get out of the way. The other team laughed and mocked us the entire time. Soon it was down to just Jeffrey and me.

"I can't believe it's just you and me," said Jeffrey, panting hard.

"Just stay behind me," I advised.

"Get that fat Jeffrey kid," yelled one of the opposing team members.

They threw the ball ten or more times without hitting either one of us. The harder they threw, the more they missed and the angrier they seemed to become.

"Okay, that's enough. You're getting too rough," yelled the teacher.

I will never forget the look on Jeffrey's face when the game ended. He could hardly believe that he had made it that far. When Jeffrey and I went to the bathroom to wash up, he was all smiles.

"Thanks for picking me first," he said.

I learned a very good lesson that day. We were just a bunch of kids who were not popular at all. Mrs. Cherry had told us that if we were to succeed in life, it wasn't just about brains or brawn. We had to learn to use all our skills, and we had to work together as a team. I just wanted to see if the teacher knew what she was talking about.

Breaking Bread

It is really cold tonight, I thought, as I pulled on the pieces of plastic and cardboard that I was using as bedcovers for the night. I shivered and shook for hours and hours as I lay inside a rusty garbage dumpster behind one of the restaurants at a shopping center in Jacksonville. I was a big kid now. If I wanted, I could smoke a whole pack of cigarettes without choking or coughing, just like a grown-up man.

"God, it's cold this time!" I said aloud.

I heard my voice echo off the sides of the dumpster, and it sounded very neat to me.

"Hello," I said, so I could hear my own echo again. "God bless America, land that I love," I sang as loud as I could.

I sound pretty darn good, I thought, continuing, "Stand beside her and guide her, through the night with a light from above."

"God! It's really cold," I said again.

I dug a hole farther down through the garbage.

When I settled down amid the smelly trash, I heard something scratching inside the dumpster.

My first thought was that it was another big rat. Several weeks earlier, I'd been bitten by one in a dumpster behind a large red brick church.

I took out my package of matches and struck one. It didn't do much to light up the dark dumpster, but now I could see that sitting in front of me was a large black cat, its green eyes shining in the darkness. It flipped his tail several times. "Meow."

"Are you hungry?" I asked.

"Meow."

I picked up the four half-eaten tacos I'd found earlier when I first climbed into the dumpster; I had been saving them for later. I unwrapped them carefully and removed bits of the hamburger for the cat. I laid the meat out on a cardboard box next to me. The cat slowly moved closer and began eating the meat. I finished off the lettuce, tomato, and cheese and threw away the taco shells, because they had coffee grounds all over the outside. When we were done, I reached up, closed the dumpster lid, and hunkered down, trying to keep myself warm. The cat moved over next to me and curled up by my neck. I began to pet its back, and it started making a sound as if it had a little motor inside.

"Do you like me?" I asked.

"Meow."

"I like you too," I said, hugging my new friend closer.

"Who's in there?!" came a holler from outside the dumpster.

The lid slowly opened, and I saw a large black man standing there with a gun in his hand.

"What you do in there?" he asked me, shaking the gun around.

"I was just sleeping, sir," I said.

"Where you live?"

"I live at an orphanage," I replied.

"Why ain't you there, then?" he asked. "You a runaway?"

I lowered my head and remained very silent. He raised his flashlight from the ground and shone it into the dumpster.

"Let me sees your face," said the man.

I covered my eyes and raised my head.

"Moves your hand, boy," he ordered.

I lowered my hand and looked toward the light.

"How comes you got a black eye?" he asked.

I said nothing.

"How long you been coming outs here, anyway?"

Still I said nothing.

"You all alone in there?" he questioned.

"No, sir. There's a black cat in here with me," I replied. "He's my friend."

"You leave that damn cat in there, and yous get out here real slow like."

I reached over and picked up the cat, held it in my arms, and began to climb out of the large garbage can.

"You don'ts listen very well, do you, boy?"

I continued climbing out of the dumpster with the cat in my arms. When I reached the ground, I hugged the cat and turned to face the man with the gun.

"You sure stink," he said, waving his hand about his nose. "How long since you had a bath?"

"I washed yesterday at the gas station."

He waved his gun to the side and told me to get in his old pickup truck.

"I gotta keep my cat. He's my friend."

"Put him in the truck," he ordered, with a strange smile on his face.

He placed the gun in his pocket and climbed into the old truck. He reached over and pushed open the passenger door so the cat and I could enter. I climbed in, and off we drove. About half an hour later, we arrived at an old house somewhere in Jacksonville. When we walked in the house, there was a kind-looking woman standing in the main room, and the man asked her to get him a towel and some soap. He took me by the arm, led me into the bathroom, and told me to get in the tub to take a bath.

"That don't means no gas station washing," he said, pointing his finger at me.

I set the cat down on the floor, and the woman came in with a towel and laid it down on the toilet. I took a hot bath and washed very well with real soap. When I was finished, I put my smelly clothes back on, picked up my cat, and walked out to the front room. The couch and the chair were full of holes, and the windows had sheets for curtains. I remember that part very well, because I had never seen anything like that before.

"Have him take his shirt off, Bill," said the woman.

"Take off your shirt," ordered the man.

I set the cat down on the couch, stood up, and began to remove my dirty shirt.

"Turns around," said the woman, spinning her finger at me in a twirling motion.

I turned around slowly and stood with my back toward them.

"You right. Someone done got this boy," said the woman.

"Who done got you?" asked the large man.

I just stood there with my head down, looking at the cat, which had lain down in one of the large holes in the couch.

"Who do this to you, boy?" asked the woman.

I stood there silently; I did not want to answer any questions. I knew very well what they were talking about. Two weeks before, I had been caught eating a box of raisins. I and some of the other boys had taken it out of the orphanage pantry while we were washing dishes from the dining room. The matron had beaten me on the breezeway porch with a stalk of bamboo because I would not tell her who took the raisins out of the locked pantry.

The man walked over to me and placed his large hand on the back of my neck.

"You hungry, boy?" he asked.

"No, sir. I had some tacos earlier tonight."

"You gonna eat, anyway."

We walked into the small kitchen and sat down at the table, which had only two chairs. I do not know exactly what it was that I ate that night, and I do not know if I ever want to know. However, it was hot, it was good, and it did not have coffee grounds stuck all over it. I stayed the night with the man and his wife. I slept on the couch with the big old holes in it, and it felt warm and good. The next day, the man drove the cat and me back to the dumpster. He handed me four whole dollars and a bag full of corn bread.

"This kind of life is better than the orphanage?" he asked.

I nodded. I opened the truck door, picked up my black cat, and said not a word. I closed the door behind me and turned around to face him. I stood there kissing my cat on the back of its neck as the man shook his head and drove away. Although it was fleeting, the warm meal, the hot bath, and the couple's concern comforted me for a long while—even to this day.

All Dressed Up and Nowhere to Go

"Excuse me. Do you have any work I could do to earn fifty cents?" I asked the shop owner.

"Why do you need fifty cents?" he wanted to know.

"I want to buy some burgers," I replied.

"Why aren't you in school this time of day?" he asked, scratching his head.

I just stood there.

"I've seen you around here a lot," he said. "You are one of those runaway kids from the orphanage over on the south side of town, ain't you?"

I nodded and replied, "I just don't like it there." I didn't mention that I'd run away with Robert and Wayne this time. They'd gone their own way, somehow.

"Don't they feed you at the orphanage?"

"Just bunches of slimy okra with a lot of hair on it, lots and lots of eggplant, and a whole bunch of bread with peanut butter and jelly all mixed together," I told him.

"Don't they feed you children any meat?"

"Yeah, we got meat, but it's got green things in it sometimes," I explained. "I don't like to eat it."

"How long have you been a runaway now?"

"Almost a week," I replied.

"Where have you been staying?" he asked, leaning up against the red brick building.

"Over in those old brick buildings by the water."

The man reached into his pocket and took out a pack of cigarettes.

"Can I have one of those?" I asked.

He handed me a cigarette.

"Have you ever gone fishing for real fish?" I asked.

I watched as he struck a match and lit his cigarette. Then he bent over and lit mine.

"You ever been fishing for real fish?" I asked again.

"Used to fish a lot when I was a kid," he said. "My daddy took me fishing all the time. I have been too busy the last few years to do any fishing." He began blowing smoke rings from his mouth, and I watched, mesmerized. "So you like to fish?" he inquired.

"Never been real fishing, except in a goldfish pond near the orphanage," I said. "I got in bad trouble, too. I got a bad beating with a bamboo stick."

"Well, I have to close up now. You ever ate pork chops?" he asked.

"What's a pork chops?"

"Let me lock up, and I'll feed you a meal you'll never forget," he said with a laugh.

I followed him around as he locked up his small shop. Then he grabbed a pile of old newspapers off his desk. We walked around the building, and I opened the passenger door to the old pickup truck. I slid in beside him and folded my hands on my lap. As we drove along, he began to sing to himself. Within five minutes, we pulled up in front of a house that was near the hospital. There was a large woman sitting on the front porch.

"You wait in the truck, until I motion for you to come up."

I nodded. He talked with the woman on the porch and she looked over at me several times. Then he waved for me to come up on the porch.

"This is my wife, Judy, and this is—hell, I don't even know your name," said the large man. "What's your name, boy?"

"Roger Dean Kiser," I told them. "That is Roger Dean Kiser with an *R, D, K*. That's my initials."

They both laughed and then sat down on the porch swing. I sat down on the cement step and watched as they talked with each other.

They let me stay at their home Friday, Saturday, and Sunday. All three nights I got to take a bath in a real bathtub. They even had yellow soap in a bottle to wash your hair. I slept in a great big bed all by myself, and we ate food that I had never seen before.

On Saturday morning, the man took me fishing on his little boat, and I caught a real fish for the very first time. When we got back to his house, his wife took me to the store and bought me a new set of clothes and a pair of cowboy boots. We looked all over for a cowboy hat, but we couldn't find one. When we got back to the house, the man gave me his old fishing hat to wear.

On Sunday, we got up early and went to church. When church was over, we ate a great big chicken dinner with cornbread and thick gravy. After lunch, the man told me that he wanted to talk with me out on the front porch.

"You can't tell anyone you were here, or I will get in serious trouble" he said sternly. "Tomorrow I will take you back to my shop, and you need to go back to the children's home. You need to stay there, and you need to go to school. That is very important. Do you understand?"

"Why can't I stay here and live with you?" I asked.

"It's against the law."

"But you ain't got nobody, and I ain't got anybody."

"Look here, son. My wife is very sick, and I have to work all the time. There is no way we can have children living here."

All the wonderful feelings I had had for three days seemed to disappear in an instant. I just sat with my head hanging down, looking at the ground.

"Would you like to go to the movies?" he asked.

"No, sir," I said quietly.

We spoke very little for the remainder of the evening. We had chicken sandwiches for supper with iced tea that had sugar cubes in it.

The next morning when I got up, I put on my new clothes and boots, and we ate breakfast. Without speaking, we started the drive back to his small shop. Suddenly he pulled off to the side of the road.

"Before I drop you off, is there anything you would like?" he asked.

"Anything?"

"What would you like?" he asked again.

"Can I have my very own pack of cigarettes?"

He pulled back onto the road, drove about a block, pulled into a gas station, and got out of the truck. I watched him as he purchased several packs of cigarettes. When he came back to the truck, he pitched them at me through his window.

Not a word was said as he and I drove back to his shop. When we arrived, we got out of the truck and walked to the front of the building. He kept looking down into my eyes as he searched for his key.

"I hope you enjoyed your stay with us," he said. "You head on back to the orphan home, and do not run away anymore. It's dangerous. You hear me?"

"Thank you for the new pants and the new shirt," I said. "I really like them a lot."

"My pleasure, boy. Now you go on back to the orphan home."

I turned and started walking toward Riverside Avenue to see if I could find Robert and Wayne, the two boys who had run away with me. When I got to the old brick building where we usually stayed, they were not there. I began walking toward the city. When I reached the downtown area, I stopped in front of one of the shops. For the longest time, I just stood looking at my reflection in the store window.

"Hey, kid. Why aren't you in school?" asked someone behind me.

I looked up and saw that it was a police officer. As usual, I spent the next two weeks in the juvenile shelter as a delinquent before I was taken back to the orphanage.

Three months later, I broke into the room where

most of our clothing was locked up, stole my new clothes, and ran away again. I searched for two days for the man's house. All I could remember was that it was over by the hospital. When I did find the house, there was no one there.

"Can I help you?" asked the neighbor, who was coming around to look at me.

"I'm looking for the man and woman who live right here," I said, pointing at the house.

"They don't live there anymore," the man said.

"Do you know where they went?"

"Look here, boy. Judy died of cancer several months back, and then old Carl—well, he shot himself a couple of days later."

I reached into my pocket, took out a cigarette, and lit it. When I opened my mouth to speak, a large smoke ring came out. I stood watching it as it circled around my head.

"It looks like you're all dressed up with nowhere to go," said the man.

I turned around and walked back to the orphanage. I didn't run away again for a long time. Whenever I wanted to run away, I'd just visit Carl and Judy in my mind and relive those three wonderful days of hot baths, a comfortable bed, and a very kind couple.

"Report to the dean's office right away," my science teacher told me when I arrived in class immediately after gym. I had no idea what I'd done, but I quickly collected my things, including my rolled-up towel, and headed down the hallway to the front office. When I arrived there, I was told to have a seat while the dean finished with the daily disciplinary reports. I sat there, wondering what I could possibly have done to be sent to the office. I could think of nothing. Several minutes later, the dean called me in.

"Please take a seat."

I sat down nervously and waited for the worst.

"Kiser," he began, "the coach asked me to have a talk with you about joining the junior varsity football squad."

I felt immediate relief that I wasn't in trouble, but the thought of playing football panicked me. "I ain't never played no football before," I told him.

"The coach is interested in your running ability. You are one of the fastest runners in the school," he explained.

"I really don't wanna play no ball. Really I don't," I told him.

The truth was, I was sure that the orphanage would never let me play on a sports team. It would be too much money for the uniform. The orphanage had never even bought me a pair of tan shorts for gym class, no matter how much I had begged. I had brown shorts, not the tan shorts I was supposed to have, and on numerous occasions I'd been chewed out in front of my class by the coach because I didn't have tan shorts like the others.

"It would be a good opportunity for you," the dean continued.

I just sat there, biting my lip and slowly shaking my head.

"Why don't you want to play?" he asked.

I wasn't sure if the dean knew that I was from the orphanage, and I was too embarrassed to tell him that it didn't allow us to play any school sports. With all the chores we had to do, the orphanage made it clear that we were not permitted to attend after-school functions—not even pep rallies. I was certain that I would never be allowed to play football.

"Let me get your file, and I'll talk it over with your parents," he said, getting up from his chair.

I panicked. "Please don't call," I said, waving my hand at him. "I'll get into bad trouble if you call and ask."

He looked puzzled. "Why would you get into trouble?"

"Please. I don't want to play no football. Really I don't."

"Something's just not right here," he said, reaching up and scratching his bald head.

I stood up from my chair and said, "Look, I live at the orphanage home. And I'll get into a lot of bad trouble if I do anything that will cost some money."

"It won't cost you anything to play on the football team," the dean stated.

"You don't understand. I have lots of work to do every day when I get home. If I don't do all my work, I'll get into real bad trouble. Real bad trouble," I told him, raising my eyebrows as high as they would go to drive my message home.

"Sit back down and wait until I get back."

I waited for about five minutes. He returned with the coach.

"Let me see your towel," said the coach.

I handed him my rolled-up towel, which hid my dirty gym shorts. He unrolled the towel, and the dark brown gym shorts fell to the floor.

"These don't look tan to me."

I gulped. "That—that's all that I can get. Honest it is. I really tried. I really did. We ain't got any tan kind of clothes at the orphanage."

The coach took my shorts and left the office. I was left standing with the dean and didn't say anything until the coach returned several minutes later with a large cardboard box.

"Here, hold these up to you and see if these will fit you," he said, throwing me a pair of tan gym shorts from the box.

I held the shorts up to my waist. "They look like they fit fine," I said with a big smile.

"We have several pairs that were left here from last year," the coach explained.

"Thank you for the right gym shorts. It makes me feel good to have the right ones now," I told him.

"Something's not right here," the coach agreed with the dean. "I don't know what it is, and I am not even sure if you know what it is. But I am going to get to the bottom of this. If you need gym shorts, Roger, you come and see me. You understand that?"

"Yes, sir!" I said and headed toward the office door. "So I don't have to join the team, right?" I asked before I left.

"Don't worry about it," he said, giving me a pat on the back.

With relief, I headed back to my science class. I was elated over the old pair of tan shorts in my hands. Finally, I would fit in at the track and just melt away into the hundreds of other tan-colored shorts. I don't know if the coach or the dean followed up on the promise to get to the "bottom of things," but the matron never said a word to me—not about the tan gym shorts nor about the fact that I no longer had the brown ones. It didn't matter; it was just good to know that they cared.

The Right and Wrong Ways to Make Twenty Bucks

I was feeling very alone as I walked along the avenue. I was hungry and cold and had nowhere to go. I had run away once again from the orphanage.

"Hey, boy!" yelled a heavyset man who was standing in the doorway of a machine shop.

"Yes, sir?" I asked.

"You want to make a couple of dollars?"

"Yes, sir!" I replied without hesitation.

"Go down to the liquor store at the end of the block and get me a pint of whiskey. Can you do that for me?" he asked.

"I can do that for two dollars," I said eagerly.

The man walked back into the shop, took a twenty-dollar bill out of the cash register, and handed it to me. I stood there looking at the large bill; I had never held that much money before. As far as I was concerned, that was all the money in the world.

I turned and walked down the block to the liquor

store. When I looked back, the man was no longer in the doorway. As soon as I turned the corner, I ran as fast as I could. It hadn't taken me long to decide I'd keep the money for myself.

Within minutes, I was blocks away from the machine shop. I sat down on a city bus bench, gasping for air. I looked at both sides of the twenty.

This will feed me for a long, long time—maybe even buy me a place to live, I thought.

Just as quickly as I had decided to keep the money, however, a new feeling, a strange one, came over me. Even to this day, I am not sure where that feeling came from. All I knew at the time was that by keeping the man's money for myself, I'd be hurting him. I sat there at the bus stop for several minutes, trying to make that feeling go away, but it would not.

I got up off the bench and ran back toward the shop. I stopped at the liquor store and purchased a pint of whiskey. I put all the change in the paper sack with the bottle and returned to the machine shop.

"I was wondering why it took you so long," said the man as I walked in.

He pulled the small bottle and the money out of the brown paper sack and handed me two dollars. I gazed down at the ground and said thank you. He patted me on the shoulder, and I walked out of his shop with the two dollars in my hand.

As I walked along the avenue, I realized that the feeling still hadn't gone away. I turned around and headed back to the machine shop. When I went inside, I walked right up to the man and held out the two dollars he had given me.

He just looked at me, and I confessed, "I was going to take all the money and not come back."

The man sighed. "But you did come back," he said. "And that is what is important."

"But I still have that bad feeling," I explained.

The man reached out, took the money from me, and stuck it in his front pocket.

"I'm going to show you how to get rid of that feeling," he said kindly.

I spent the rest of the day cleaning up his shop. I cut myself several times on the metal shavings I picked up off the floor. By the end of the day, I was covered in bandages from the tips of my fingers to my elbows. At around seven o'clock, he called me into his little office.

"Let's see now. You worked ten hours today. At two dollars and twelve cents an hour, that's twenty-one dollars and twenty cents."

I held out my bandaged hand as he counted the money.

"Am I still a stealer?" I asked.

"You are not a stealer, boy. Not by a long shot," he said with a smile, and I smiled back.

After leaving the machine shop, I stopped every block or so to see if that bad feeling would come back, but it never did. During the next fifteen years, I returned to that machine shop every now and again to help or to have some lunch. That man became my friend, and I am so thankful that he took the time to teach me that there was a right way to make twenty dollars—and a little change, to boot.

Donald's Mother

I met Donald one evening as he was walking through a back alley. I had been living in the alley for almost a week. I was standing next to a dumpster, raking my finger around the inside of a nearly empty tuna can.

"You ain't eating that, are you?" he asked, stopping in front of me.

A little embarrassed, I tossed the empty tin into the dumpster.

"If you're hungry, I'll take you over to my house, and I'll get my mom to fix you something to eat."

He turned and began walking away. I followed him, several paces behind.

Donald was a much taller boy than I was, but I could tell that he was about twelve, right around my age. I had a hard time keeping up with him because his legs were so long.

After walking for about half an hour, he stopped in front of an old corner house. I stood there, looking at the old board structure with its peeling white paint. I had seen old houses before, but this was really old, like a shack. I looked at Donald to see if he might be playing a joke on me or something. Then the front door opened, and there stood an old woman, bent over at a forty-five-degree angle.

"Mom, this is Roger. He's hungry," Donald told the woman.

"Roger, you come on in this house right this minute, and let's see what we can find you to eat," she said.

I followed the two of them into the house, looking in every direction as I walked. Donald and I stopped in the living room, and his mother headed toward the back of the house.

The house was very dark inside. There was only one light in the front room, hanging from the center of the ceiling by an old green cord. I stood watching as Donald screwed the bulb into the socket, giving us light.

"Have a seat," he told me.

I had the choice of a few ratty couches and a large stuffed chair in the corner, but it had no seat, just old black springs and some cotton stuff.

Donald walked toward a dark room behind the living room and said, "I'll be right back. I have to use the bathroom."

I sat down on the edge of one of the couches and watched as he pulled a curtain across the doorway. Finding that strange, I looked around and realized that none of the doorways actually had doors. Something flashed in the corner of my eye, and I looked toward it. I could actually see cars whizzing by through the wallboards. *These here walls ain't got any insides to 'em*, I thought.

When Donald returned, he suggested that we sit on the front porch. I liked the thought of that, since it was so dark in the house. We sat on the weathered patio and watched the traffic. A few moments later, Donald's mother came out.

"Here you go, young man," she said, handing me a large plate of fried potatoes and a thin slice of bread.

I had not had anything hot to eat for a week. I gobbled up the food. When I finished the entire plate in under three minutes, the thought occurred to me that they must think I'm a pig. My face grew hot.

"Would you like more?" Donald's mother asked.

"No, thank you, ma'am. I had plenty," I replied, even though I probably could have eaten more.

I was invited to stay the night, and it was a relief that I didn't have to go back to the alley that evening. For supper, we again had fried potatoes and a slice of bread. There were no pots, so that daily meal had to be fried on the old metal stovetop and then mashed down until the potatoes were done.

His mother slept on a small army cot in the corner of the kitchen, and Donald and I slept on an old stained mattress on the living room floor. I was awake for hours, watching the traffic through the wallboards.

Donald's mother was up early, getting ready to go to work. Donald had told me that she worked at the Goodwill store. I did not know how she could work at a job, because she walked as though she were crippled. It took her a long time to even get from one side of the living room to the other, much less walk to the bus stop and catch a bus to work.

"Donald, you make sure you go to school today, son," she told him as she hobbled out the front door.

Several minutes after she left, Donald got up and began getting ready for school. I was already dressed because I had slept in my clothes. I folded the small mattress in half and walked out to the front porch to wait for my friend.

As he walked out on the porch, he told me that I could stay at their house until he got out of school at 3:30 PM. Then he walked down the street and disappeared around the corner.

I sat on the porch for several hours before I went back into the house to use the bathroom. When I had finished, I began to walk around the house. It was a small three-room dump, with white peeling paint that dropped off in large pieces each time the front door slammed. It had a dirty-looking structure, with light brown pieces of cardboard boxes stuck here and there in the window frames. Looking around the kitchen, I saw that there was hardly any food. There were several bags of potatoes in the corner, and some of them were rotten. There were four or five cans of beans and a can of carrots sitting on an old wooden shelf. In the refrigerator, there was some cheese and a jar of pickles. I opened the small freezer and found one small package of frozen meat.

I walked back out onto the porch and sat there wondering. I couldn't figure out why people would share their food with me when they had so little for themselves.

Suddenly a lightbulb went off, and I jumped up and ran down the street until I came to the local grocery store. I walked right up to the man at the meat counter and said, "I need to get some real good meat, and I need it really bad, too. I'll work hard for it, I really will," I told him.

The man reached over, picked up a white apron, and tossed it to me. I caught it and looked at him expectantly.

"Get your butt behind the counter and get to work," he said with a smile.

For five hours, I cleaned counters, shined glass, and mopped floors. At two o'clock, I told the man that I had to go. He wiped his hands on his apron and asked, "How much do I owe you?"

"I don't want no money. I just want food and meat."

"Why do you want food? You're just a kid."

"I got a friend who don't have much food, and his mom is real crippled like. She walks funny, and I need the food for them."

Although I had probably earned less than five dollars, the butcher gave me almost twenty dollars' worth of meat and canned goods. When Donald got home from school, I was waiting for him on the porch. I did not say anything to him about the groceries, and we headed to the park to watch the ducks swimming in the small pond. By the time his mother got home from work, Donald and I were waiting for her on the porch. She hobbled up onto the porch, smiled at me, and sat down. She opened her purse and took out several dollars.

"Son, you and Roger walk down to the grocery

store and get us a small package of hamburger for supper."

"There's a hamburger pack in the refrigerator," I told her.

"Well, that's strange. I ain't bought hamburger meat in a long while," she said, getting up from her chair and walking into the house.

About a minute later, Donald and I walked inside to get out of the sun. I looked up when I heard Donald's mother coming out of the kitchen. She had tears in her eyes.

"What's wrong, Mom?" Donald asked.

"Oh, God, did you boys steal all this food?"

"I was in school all day!" Donald cried, looking at me.

His mother looked at me, too.

I gulped. "I worked at the grocery store all day, and the butcher paid in groceries," I explained.

Donald's mother sat down on the end of the couch and cried for several minutes. Donald and I just sat there, our hands folded on our laps, having no idea what we should do. That evening, I watched Donald and his mother scarf down their food in much the same way I had eaten the potatoes and bread the day before.

Before bedtime, Donald's mother and I had a long talk out on the porch. I told her that I had run away from the orphanage and that I had no place to stay.

"Thank you for the wonderful dinner," she told me. She wrapped her arms around me and squeezed as tightly as she could. It felt good to be held, and I suddenly felt a sense of worth to someone. I felt needed.

When she let me go, I looked at her and said, "If you will let me stay here, I will take care of you."

Once again, tears welled up in her eyes. Donald stuck his head out the doorway to see what was happening.

"You can stay here, and you don't have to take care of me," she said.

Donald came all the way out to the patio to hug his mom. And I just smiled. I stayed with Donald and his mother for almost four months before I figured it was time to move on. I didn't have much to contribute, and they had so little that I felt I should set off on my own and make my own way. I was back at the juvenile shelter before long, but I always remembered the time that I spent with Donald and his mother.

Bighearted Betsy

HELP WANTED. NO EXPERIENCE NECESSARY read the large hand-painted sign that was stuck in the dirt along the side of the road.

"Wow!" I said as I read it, and I hurried up the quarter-mile driveway and knocked at the first house I came to, hoping that the job was still available.

"Can I help you?" asked the large man who opened the door.

"I'm here about the no-experience job."

"How old are you?"

"About fourteen, sir," I replied.

"Where do you live?"

"I got no home, sir. No family."

"Have you ever worked on a dairy before?"

"No, sir. I have never had a real job before."

"My name is Don. What kind of jobs have you done?" he asked.

"Just criminal kinds of stuff."

"Criminal stuff? Are you a criminal?" he questioned.

"That's what the reform school told me," I said, looking down at the ground.

"What did you do to be sent to the reformatory?"

"Just running away from the orphanage and that kind of stuff."

"Do you know anything about working on a dairy?"

"I know about cows and stuff like that."

"What do you know about cows?"

"You squeeze them on the bottom and white milk comes out."

"Well, kid, I guess you got the job," said Don.

We walked over to an old white shack. He said it was mine to live in for as long as I worked at the dairy. Then he gave me a pair of old rubber boots and some gloves.

"You got any belongings?" he asked.

"What are belongings?"

"Things," he said.

"Things?" I repeated.

"Stuff, clothes, and money," he explained, waving his hand over his head, pushing his hair out of his eyes.

"I ain't got any clothes and stuff, and I sure ain't got any money," I admitted.

He pulled out his wallet and handed me five dollars.

"Go down to the store and get yourself some food. There are pots and pans in the cupboard. I'll take this from your salary."

He walked out the door.

"At 4:00 AM I'll be knocking on your door, so be ready," he yelled back at me.

I walked to the store and purchased a package of hot dogs, a loaf of bread, and a bottle of catsup. Returning to the old shack, I got a pan of water and boiled the hot dogs. This was the first time I'd ever cooked for myself. Only one of the hot dogs split on the side, so I knew I was going to be a good cook. Then I walked around for a while, in my very first house, before going to bed.

"Up and at 'em!" someone yelled before beating on my front door.

I jumped out of bed. My heart was racing fifty miles an hour. I stood up and looked around the room, wondering where I was.

"Get a move on! Get those rubber boots on and get them cows into the barn," yelled the stranger.

Four AM, cows, milk? What the heck is going on here? I wondered.

As I dressed, it all came back to me. I was a man now.

I had a job, a house, and hot dogs to eat. I had to go to work to make money. I walked over to the window and looked outside. I saw no need for rubber boots when it was not raining. I locked my front door with my very own key and walked toward the large barn.

"Open that gate and run those cows into the barn," yelled one of the two men who were standing in the darkness.

I opened the gate and then closed it behind me. Waving my arms, I ran around behind the cattle so they would move into the barn. I might not have been the brightest kid on the block, but it took me very little time to understand what those rubber boots were for. I'd always thought that stuff on the ground at dairies was just mud that didn't smell too good.

We had to milk the cows twice a day, seven days a week, and work from sunup to sundown. After the first few days, I was almost dead from exhaustion.

The next morning, I got up and walked out to the barn about 2:00 AM. The boss had bought several dozen doughnuts the night before, and I'd taken them to my house for supper. I stood by the fence, eating one, when a black and white cow walked right up to me and stood there. I pulled off a piece of doughnut and held it out. To my surprise, she gently took it from my hand and ate it.

After that, that cow would always be waiting for me each morning when I came out of my shack. I made sure that I kept plenty of doughnuts at all times so that she and I could share breakfast.

I noticed that she had a large black heart shape on her side, so I named her Bighearted Betsy. I would take one small bite of the doughnut and then give the rest to her. We did that every day that I worked there.

I was in the barn about two weeks later when the boss yelled for me to come over to his house. When I arrived, he sat down at his kitchen table and said, "Bad news, kid."

"What kinda bad news?"

"Things are bad around here. Got to close the dairy in about a week," he told me.

"Cows are giving good milk, Don," I said.

"There's a lot more to the damn dairy business than just the milk," he replied, shaking his head.

"Do I lose my shack?"

"Afraid so, kid. You finish out the week, and I'll pay you then. You were a hard-working criminal kid," he said, as he laughed, turned his back toward me, and wiped his face on a handkerchief, "so I'll give you a little something extra at the end of the week."

I walked out of the office and returned to the silo,

where I finished shoveling the sour hay that was stored there. Later that afternoon, I saw a bunch of men driving up in an old pickup truck. They took a bunch of tools out of the back of the truck and carried them to the far end of the barn.

"What's all them tools gonna do?" I hollered at one of the men.

He didn't say anything, but he drew a finger across his throat like a knife, and then he laughed. I didn't think anything more about it until I got up the next morning. I did not see the big silver milk truck, which always came to collect the milk.

I walked out of my shack and did not see Bighearted Betsy at the corral fence. I was surprised when I saw that all the cows were already in the barn and in the stalls. I stuck the doughnut in my front pocket and headed toward the barn at a very fast pace. I wanted to know who was doing my job when it was mine to do.

All of a sudden a strange man grabbed me by the arm.

"Where you headed, kid?"

"Someone's doing my job."

The man grabbed me again, turned me around, and pushed me out the barn door.

"You go on back to where you came from. This ain't a place for a kid."

"But I work here for Don, and I got to help milk," I yelled.

"Ain't any milk'n around here no more," said the large man. "We're getting ready to slaughter."

"What's a slaughter?"

"Going to turn them into meat steaks."

"You mean kill 'em all?" I yelled.

"That's life, kid. Get used to it," he said, as he turned and walked away.

"You ain't going to shoot them? Are you?"

He stopped, turned around, and walked back toward me.

"How old are you, boy?"

"Fourteen, I think."

"Okay, you want to know the truth?" he said, looking directly into my eyes.

"Yes, sir."

"They line them up and hit each cow on the head with a sledgehammer, and then they cut their throats."

I stood there in a state of shock.

"But these here are milk cows, not meat cows," I replied, lowering my head and looking down at the ground.

"All cows are meat cows, kid. Got to go and get it done."

He gave me a look of concern and walked away.

I kept standing there. As the man disappeared, I walked into the barn and found Bighearted Betsy among the herd. I released her steel bar and backed her out of the stall. She followed me out to the corral. I hugged her neck and then I took the doughnut out of my pocket and gave it to her. I turned around, walked out of the corral, went back to my shack, and began packing my few belongings. When I walked back out the front door, Betsy was standing where she always stood every morning since I met her.

"Moo," she bellowed.

I slowly walked back over to the fence and reached out to pet her for the last time. Lying on the ground was one small piece of doughnut, which she had not eaten.

She bellowed again.

I reached down, picked up the small piece of doughnut, and held it out to her, but she refused it. I pushed it toward her mouth again, and again she refused to eat it.

"Moo," she cried, as she slobbered and shook her head back and forth.

"I can't do it," I told her.

"Moo," she went again.

I took the small piece of doughnut and raised it to my lips. I opened my mouth, inserted the one bite of cake, and began to chew. I swallowed the piece of doughnut and stood there crying. Betsy snorted, turned around, and started walking toward the barn. She never looked back, and she finally disappeared into the large doorway.

I grabbed my small bag of clothes, my gloves, and my rubber boots. I walked over to Don's house and knocked on the door. When the door opened, I held out my gloves and my boots.

"I don't want to work here no more," I told him.

"Come on inside," he motioned with his head.

I walked in and sat down at the kitchen table.

"What do I owe you?"

"Can I have a cow instead of money and maybe that extra that you were going to give me?" I asked.

"And just what are you going to do with a damn cow?" he questioned.

"I thought I would make her like my horse."

"Look, kid, I am going to save you a lot of grief. Just take this money and forget it," he ordered, as he handed me an envelope.

"They're going to kill all the cows, anyway."

"Get your butt out to my truck, and I'll carry you

out to the highway," he said, pointing at the door.

I got up from the chair, walked out the door, and got into his truck. He drove me down the long driveway to the road and told me to get out. He spun around and headed back up the driveway to the barn. I stood there for about thirty minutes, with nothing but the wind and the light bleeding into the morning sky and the occasional sound of a distant car going somewhere. Then I turned and slowly started walking down the highway, thinking I'd seen my last of that farm.

Several miles later, I began to hitchhike. Many cars passed before a truck finally stopped and offered me a ride. Little did I know that it was one of the men who had slaughtered the cattle.

"Did you get any meat?" asked the man.

"I don't want any meat."

"I got some in the back if you want some."

I looked through the back window of the truck and saw ten or fifteen packages of meat wrapped in shiny white plastic paper. We had driven for about ten miles when the man told me he had to turn off at the next crossing.

"I'll just get off at the corner," I said.

"Well, I got to pee, anyway. Watch my truck, and

I'll be back in a minute," he said as he ran off the road and into a wooded area.

I walked to the back of the truck and looked at the packages lying in the back. I reached out and felt one of the packages, but I jerked my hand back when I felt the package's warmth. I saw that one package had a note stuck to it that read "Mark, Lilly phoned and said for you to please pick up some bread, milk, and doughnuts on your way home." I removed the note from the package and stuck it on one of the other packages. Then I took the package that had had the note attached to it and threw it into the bushes along the side of the road.

Several minutes later, the man returned. I thanked him for the ride, and he drove away. I walked out into the bushes and picked up the shiny white package. I got down on my hands and knees and dug a deep hole in the hard ground. Then I buried "Betsy" next to a tree, right by the big ditch.

A Most Wonderful Woman

For several months after I was released from reform school, I was locked up in the juvenile hall. I refused to return to the orphanage, even if I had to spend the rest of my life in a small cage. I flatly refused to walk out the front door of the juvenile hall to help them clean up the streets for fear that they would take me back to that awful place. So when Burt, a man who worked for the court, came into my cell one Wednesday morning and asked if I wanted to go somewhere special for Thanksgiving dinner, I told him that I did not want to go. I liked Burt, so I listened to him go on and on about how great a Thanksgiving dinner would be and how a kid should not be locked up on Thanksgiving. He was so persistent that I finally gave in.

Later that afternoon, a woman, Mrs. Usher, came to the shelter. She said that Burt had mentioned me to her, then she talked with me for about ten minutes and told me that she wanted to take me to her house for Thanksgiving dinner the next day. I made her promise that she would bring me back the day after, and she promised. So I went with her.

We arrived at her nice home, and I sat very still on a chair in the living room while dozens of people came and went, preparing for the big Thanksgiving dinner. I felt so out of place that I wanted to go right back to the juvenile hall and back to the shelter of my cage. I stayed very still until much later in the afternoon when most of the people had left.

When Mrs. Usher offered me a Coca-Cola in the small bottle, I politely declined, even though I wanted it really bad. I was just too scared to accept it. I thought about that Coke throughout the day and how good it would have tasted. So later that night, when everyone was asleep, I snuck into the kitchen slowly and quietly and took a cold Coca-Cola out of the refrigerator. I gulped it down within seconds and hid the bottle cap behind the refrigerator. Then I pressed the empty bottle against my stomach to warm it up like the other discarded ones. I hoped that no one would find out that I had drunk it.

The following day, Thanksgiving Day, was more unbearable than the day before. Having all these strange people around me, laughing with one another and looking at me with sad eyes, embarrassed me. I was scared, not like scared-of-the-dark scared, but scared in a different kind of way. I couldn't quite put my finger on it. Even though I had never seen so much food in all my life, I could hardly eat. When dinner was finally over, I sure was glad.

When the dishes had been cleared and all the guests had left, Mrs. Usher invited me to sit with her on the front porch. She asked me questions about myself and my life, and she entertained me with stories of her own life. We talked for hours and hours. I had never spent so much one-to-one time with such a nice person, and I really liked it. However, even her kindness and warmth could not make me trust her completely. I could not understand why she wanted me to come to her house and spend time with her. I was suspicious, so I kept one eye on her at all times.

Mrs. Usher excused herself and went in the house. When she returned, she was holding two small bottles of Coke. Smiling, she handed me one, and I was grateful. The bottle was cold in my palm, and when I drank the Coke, it tasted so wonderful that the taste has stayed with me all this time. That was the best Coke I ever drank in my entire life.

The next morning we had breakfast together, and then she told me to gather my things so that she could take me back to the hall, as she had promised. While I was getting my few belongings together, I heard her on the telephone. She was talking to the authorities, demanding to know why they were going to send me back to the reform school. She wanted to know what I did that was so bad that I had to be sent back there. She became very irate and said that she wouldn't bring me back to be caged up like an animal and that I was a boy who deserved to be treated with kindness.

My heart swelled with love when I heard Mrs. Usher say that. She made me feel worth something, able to become somebody someday. I ended up staying with the Ushers for several weeks, and even after I had to go on my way to the next stop, I continued to see them on and off for the next twenty or so years, until their deaths.

I loved that woman, and I wish I could have shown her just how much, but I did not know how to express it. Now that Mrs. Usher is in heaven, I know that she knows how much I love and respect her. Her kindness lifted the spirits of one lonely little boy, and perhaps this lonely little boy lifted her spirits as well. I hope so.

The Most Honest Man I Ever Knew

Throughout my life, I have met many men, both good and bad, but of all those men, there is one who stands out from the others. I met him the Wednesday afternoon that Mrs. Usher took me out of the juvenile shelter to share Thanksgiving dinner with her and her family.

The gray-haired gentleman didn't say a word when I walked in the house. He just looked me over and then headed into the dining room. He was Mrs. Usher's husband. The more familiar I became to him, the more he had to say, but there still wasn't a lot of talking going on between us. He was just a quiet type of fellow, and I accepted that about him.

One of the times that I was out running the streets, I telephoned Mr. Usher, and he immediately drove over and picked me up from a very bad part of town. I was grateful that I had him to turn to.

Mr. Usher was in construction, so he made arrangements to pay me for picking up scraps at one of his construction sites. Although I had known Mr. Usher for quite some time by then, I learned much more about him from the men who worked with him. At lunch, while sitting on concrete blocks or dirt piles, the workers would speak very highly of Mr. Usher. They said he was the most wonderful, kind man they had ever known.

Over the years, Mr. Usher always seemed to be available if I needed anything. He and his wife often took me into their home for a few weeks at a time. I would answer the telephone and take messages for Mr. Usher when he wasn't available. The number of calls he received from people wanting his construction services was amazing. I couldn't understand why they were so particular about who built their buildings.

One day Mr. Usher asked me to go to a construction site in Georgia with him for a few weeks. He was building a new Burger King restaurant, and since I had nothing better to do then than run the back streets, I accepted.

As I worked on the site, I watched him very closely. He never seemed to get upset, even if something major went wrong. He expertly managed every aspect of construction, including the payroll. Every board, every screw, every nail, and every shingle was accounted for. Nothing useful was scrapped or thrown away. One afternoon I asked him why everything was so important to him. He explained that wasting materials on someone else's dollar was the same as stealing from them.

One Friday night, as we were heading back to Jacksonville for a weekend of rest, we stopped for gas. When he saw that he had unwittingly taken a box of nails and a hammer from the work site, we drove back the way we had come, which took well over half an hour, to return the hammer and the nails to the construction site. When we were back on our way to Jacksonville, I asked him why he didn't just wait until Monday to return the hammer and the nails. That's when I realized that Mr. Usher was the most honest man I knew.

He said, "If you want to be an honest person, you have to work at it. Being bad is easy, but being honest is hard and sometimes very difficult. I suppose I could have waited until Monday to return the property. However, I had to make a choice. I could be a thief for only thirty minutes or I could be a thief for the entire weekend. I chose the shortest amount of time. You have to remember, Roger, it is not *who* we are in this world but *what* we are in this world that is important."

It took me years to understand what Mr. Usher was really talking about. It wasn't about the hammer and the nails at all. It was all about honesty. It was about being fair to others and about what other people think of you as a person—that each person can determine what to become based on the decisions that he or she makes on a daily basis. I guess honesty was more important to him than taking a hammer, a nail, or an office stamp, even by accident.

I learned from him that being honest is something that requires very hard work. Honesty earns you respect. To him, honesty and respect were more important than anything else.

I had always thought that there were different degrees of honesty and that a person could only be as honest as the environment in which he lived. I was an honest boy, or so I thought. I was good and I was honest, at least until I became hungry and had no money for food.

Mr. Usher was always neat and clean in appearance. He was always excellently groomed, whether he was going to church or to work. He was not a vain man. He always took the time to groom himself because of his respect for others. "If others honor me by accepting me in their presence, I must always show my respect for them by being neat and clean," he told me.

Near the end of his life, I visited Mr. Usher at the hospital. As he lay in the hospital bed in a coma, he looked terrible. Out of respect for him, I closed my eyes as I spoke to him. I do not know if he could hear me. Almost in tears, I told him that he was the only man on Earth whom I had allowed to have my respect. I said that I would give him my heart, but the juvenile judge told me that I didn't have one.

When he died, I cried. It was one of the few times in my life that I have ever shed tears over the loss of a person. I will forever remember the man I was honored to call my foster father. He was truly the most honest man I ever met.

A Full-Fledged Cowboy

"Silt, Colorado!" hollered the Greyhound bus driver as he pulled off to the side of the road. I grabbed my small bag and climbed off the bus. At the side of the road was a large man standing beside an old army jeep.

"Are you Roger Kiser?" he asked.

"Yes, sir," I replied.

"My name is Owen Boulton. I own the Rainbow K Ranch," he said, as he stuck out his hand to shake mine.

The juvenile judge in Florida had sent me to Colorado to work on a ranch. It was a program set up to help troubled teenagers. Within a week I became a full-fledged cowboy. I was assigned a large horse named Brownie and was given a full outfit of western wear as well as a list of duties, which started at around four o'clock each morning.

Things went rather well for the first couple of

months. We worked from 4:00 AM until 6:00 PM, seven days a week. We bailed hay, branded cattle, collected chicken eggs, mended fences, and shoveled cow manure. It was a never-ending job. The best part was my horse, Brownie. In addition to my other chores, it was my job to care for her. I fed, bathed, and brushed her down on a daily basis.

Every morning, when I came out to collect the eggs from the chicken coop, she was waiting for me by the gate. I would walk over and pet her on her side. She would toss her head backward and make a strange sound, as though she was blowing through her lips. Slobber flew everywhere.

"I bet you could sure whistle loud, if you had some hands," I told her.

She stomped her feet and turned around in a circle.

After we ranch hands ate our breakfast, I was told that I would have to go with several of the older men to repair fences up on the northern range. We loaded the jeep with materials and tools, and off we went. It was almost 7:00 PM when we got back to the ranch. As we drove up to the barn, I saw about twenty ranch hands sitting around in a circle. I got out of the jeep and walked toward them.

"What's going on?" I asked.

"It's your horse, Brownie. She's dead," said one of the men.

Slowly, I walked over to where Brownie was lying in the corral. I bent down and petted her on her side. It took everything I had to keep from crying in front of all those men. Suddenly the corral gate opened and Mr. Boulton came riding in on an old tractor. He began scooping out a large hole right next to Brownie.

"What's he going to do?" I yelled.

"We always bury the horses right where they drop," said one of the ranch hands.

I stood to the side while he dug the hole for Brownie. I wiped the tears as they rolled down my cheeks. I will never forget that feeling of sadness for as long as I live.

When a large hole had been dug, the men stood back so that Brownie could be moved into it. Mr. Boulton lowered the large tractor scoop and moved toward Brownie.

"Please, Mr. Boulton! Please don't move Brownie with that tractor bucket. You'll cut her and mess her up!" I yelled.

I ran in front of the tractor, waiving my arms up in the air.

"Look here, boy," said Mr. Boulton. "We have no

choice but to do this when a horse dies. She is just too heavy to move by hand."

"I'll get her in the hole. I swear I will, Mr. Owen, sir," I shouted.

I ran over to Brownie and pushed on her head as hard as I could, but she barely moved. I pushed and pushed as hard as I could, but her body was just too heavy. Nothing I tried would move her any closer toward the hole. Finally, I stopped and just sprawled in the dirt, with my head resting against Brownie's side.

"Please don't use that bucket scoop on Brownie," I said over and over.

One at a time, the ranch hands got off their horses. Each positioned himself around the large brown horse, and they began to push and pull with all their might. Inch by inch, Brownie moved toward the large hole in the ground. Suddenly she slid downhill. I raised her head as best I could so that her face would not scar. The next thing I knew, I was being pulled down into the hole.

Suddenly everything went totally silent. I just sat there at the bottom of the hole with Brownie's head resting on my lap. Dust and dirt was settling all around me. I slowly got to my feet and placed her head flat on the ground. Then I positioned her legs so they were straight. I removed my western shirt and placed it over her face so that dirt would not get into her eyes.

I stood there, crying, as my best friend was covered with dirt. Most of that night, I stayed in the barn and cleaned Brownie's stall. I cried until I could cry no more. I guess I was just too embarrassed to go back to the bunkhouse with the rest of the ranch hands.

Early the next morning, I walked back to the bunkhouse to shower and change my clothes before going out to collect the eggs. As I entered the small wooden house, the ranch hands were up and getting dressed. Lying on my bunk was eight dollars and some change. On a matchbook cover was written "Buy yourself a new shirt."

When I looked up, all the men were smiling at me. One of them said, "You may be a city boy, R. D."— that's what they always called me—"but you definitely have the heart that it takes to be a real honest-to-goodness cowboy."

I wiped my swollen red eyes and smiled proudly.

When I was about fifteen, the juvenile court—having no idea what else to do with me—sent me to live at a boardinghouse that was just a block or so from the juvenile shelter. The court covered the cost of my small room for four weeks and set me up with a job at Murphy's Heating and Sheet Metal Shop, which was about four miles from the boardinghouse. Since I had no transportation, one of the older men who worked there offered to give me a ride to and from work every day in exchange for several dollars a week. Unfortunately, this man often missed at least one or two days of work each week. So on the days he didn't go, I was on my own. By the time I would walk the four miles to the shop, the men had usually already loaded up the trucks and left. Each time this happened, the head boss would send me home.

On the days I worked, it was the same routine. I would return to the boardinghouse afterward, change my clothes, and walk to a nearby hamburger joint to get myself something to eat. After eating, I would walk the five miles or so to a small local park. This was an area of town where my friends and I would gather throughout the years whenever we ran away from the orphanage.

On some days, no one would show up at all, and I would sit there for hours all by myself. On other days, one or two of my friends would come to the park, and we would roam the back streets together.

"Do you know what time the next bus comes?" asked someone behind me.

As I turned around, I noticed a young girl about my age standing behind the park bench.

"No, ma'am. I don't know anything about the buses. There's a bunch of them that come by all the time, though," I responded.

The girl sat down on the bench beside me, and we began to talk. For the next hour she told me about her family, and I told her about my life in the orphanage and the reform school. She and I talked on and on about the schools we attended. I was a rather shy boy, and I was quite surprised that someone as pretty as she would want to sit and talk to someone like me.

"You sure are awful nice, and you talk real nice, too," she said.

I sat there smiling from ear to ear. I could not believe that this was happening to me. It wasn't possible that someone like her thought that I was smart or worth talking to.

Suddenly I saw my two friends Donald and Johnny walking across the street.

"There are my friends coming right there," I told her. "Can you do something extra special for me?"

"What's that?" she questioned.

"Those are my friends, and they both got girlfriends. Can you tell them that you are my girlfriend? I don't mean like a real girlfriend. I know you can't say anything like that. But I mean like a girl who's my friend."

She smiled at me and then nodded her head. By then both Donald and Johnny had arrived.

"You're sure here early today," said Donald.

"I didn't work again today. I didn't have a ride."

Both Donald and Johnny were now looking at the girl.

"Oh, this is, uh, this is Judy. She's, uh—she's, uh," I stuttered.

"Hi, I'm Judy. I'm Roger's new girlfriend," she blurted out. She then slid over next to me and placed her arm on my shoulder.

Both Johnny and Donald's eyes got very big. I

looked over at Judy and thanked her with my eyes.

I cannot tell you how wonderful that made me feel as a young boy. For that moment in time, everything in the world was wonderful and beautiful. I was so proud that my friends would now know that a girl liked me.

"Well, we're going to the movies. You two want to go?" asked Johnny.

"I've got to be home by six o'clock," Judy said.

"It's just before four now. You got time," Johnny told her. "If you guys want to go, we'll meet you over there."

Johnny and Donald walked away and headed toward the theater, which was about half a block away from the park.

"I got some money, if you want to go to the movie," I told Judy, as I held out a dollar bill. "I'll pay for the movie and give you this whole dollar for your time."

"Why would you want to pay someone to go to the movies with you?"

"I don't mean anything bad. I really don't," I told her.

She sat there looking at me somewhat strangely.

The four of us went to the movie, and we had a wonderful time. It was the first time in my life that I had ever sat that close to a girl.

After the movie, the four of us walked to the bus stop and waited for the bus to take Judy home. As the bus was pulling up, Judy looked over at me. Then she looked over at Donald and Johnny, who were both staring at me. I stood there, not having the slightest idea of what to do.

"Later, Rog," said Judy. Then she turned and walked toward me.

"Bye," I said, as I barely raised my hand.

Judy walked over and kissed me on the cheek, and then she hugged me very quickly.

"Whoa," said Johnny, as he slapped me on the back. "How long has this been going on?"

I stood in shock, unable to speak, silently watching as the bus lights disappeared into the darkness.

I will forever remember Judy and that day. She was a very kind young woman who was able to read between the lines, even though she was looking at a blank piece of paper.

This Here Money

On the way home from my job at Murphy's Heating and Sheet Metal Shop, I happened upon a small wood-frame house that was in full flames. Standing out in the street was a woman, her arms wrapped around three small children. Next to her was a man who was down on his knees, his hands covering his face and his body wracked by sobs. Within minutes, the fire trucks arrived, along with people running from every direction. I stood watching as the small wooden house finally collapsed on itself.

"Do you live here?" a police officer asked me.

"No, sir. I think that woman and man do," I told him, pointing toward the couple.

The officer walked over and began to question the family.

Within thirty minutes, the fire was out, and there was nothing left of the house except smoldering embers.

"What's we gonna do?" the woman asked the man, as she too began to cry.

The man just stood there, shaking his head back and forth.

"We got nowhere to go," the woman yelled out at her children, as she began hugging them.

"I got this here room at the rooming house," I told them. "You can stay there for tonight. I'm sure it will be all right."

The woman said something to the man, and within several minutes the six of us were walking toward my rooming house. When we arrived, my landlady was out on the front porch. As we walked up onto the deck, I could see from the look in her eyes that something was not right. She told the family to sit down on the wooden chairs, and she asked me to come with her.

As we walked down the hallway, I explained to her that the family had nowhere to go—that their house had burned down and they would have to sleep outside in the cold.

"There is no way that they can stay here. Those people are Negroes. Can't you see that, young man?"

"But they got nowhere to go."

"That's not my problem, and it's certainly not your problem."

READER/CUSTOMER CARE SURVEY

HEMG

We care about your opinions! Please take a moment to fill out our online Reader Survey at **http://survey.hcibooks.com**. As a **"THANK YOU"** you will receive a **VALUABLE INSTANT COUPON** towards future book purchases as well as a **SPECIAL GIFT** available only online! Or, you may mail this card back to us.

First Name _____ MI. _____ Last Name _____

Address _____ Zip _____ Email _____

State _____ City _____

1. Gender
- ☐ Female ☐ Male

2. Age
- ☐ 8 or younger
- ☐ 9-12
- ☐ 17-20
- ☐ 31+

☐ 13-16
☐ 21-30

3. Did you receive this book as a gift?
- ☐ Yes ☐ No

4. Annual Household Income
- ☐ under $25,000
- ☐ $25,000 - $34,999
- ☐ $35,000 - $49,999
- ☐ $50,000 - $74,999
- ☐ over $75,000

5. What are the ages of the children living in your house?
_____
_____
_____

6. Marital Status
- ☐ Single
- ☐ Married
- ☐ Divorced
- ☐ Widowed

Comments
_____
_____
_____
_____
_____

BUSINESS REPLY MAIL

FIRST-CLASS MAIL PERMIT NO 45 DEERFIELD BEACH, FL

POSTAGE WILL BE PAID BY ADDRESSEE

Health Communications, Inc.
3201 SW 15th Street
Deerfield Beach FL 33442-9875

"But what are they going to do?" I inquired.

"Look at me," she said, cocking her head to one side. "It's not your problem, and there is nothing we can do for them. Now you go out there, and you tell those people they have to leave," she continued.

I turned around slowly and walked back down the hallway. That was the longest walk I have ever had to walk. Halfway down the hallway, I stopped and looked back.

"Come here for a minute," she told me.

I followed her to the door that led into her room. I stood outside while she went in. Several minutes later, she returned and handed me five dollars.

"Give this to that family and tell them that's the best we can do."

"Can I see if anyone else will give a little money?" I asked.

"Just this one time, but don't you be doing this anymore. Okay?"

"Okay," I said with a grin.

As fast as I could, I traveled from door to door, telling the story of the family that had lost everything. From twenty-eight rooms, I raised almost sixty dollars. When I had finished I walked back to the landlady's room and showed her the money.

"I am really surprised," she said, shaking her head back and forth.

"You see, there *was* something we could do," I told her. "All we had to do is keep trying real hard."

"You are something else, Roger Kiser."

I walked back to the front porch and explained to the family that it was against the rules for me to allow anyone to stay in my room.

"There ain't any black people living here, so all this here money came from white people. They all feel real bad that you ain't got no place to go," I told them, as I held out the handful of money.

"Everyone who lives here gave money?" asked the man.

"Everyone who was in their rooms."

"Can you tell them that they get a free shoe shine if they come down to the Trailways bus station?" he replied.

As far as I know, no one ever went to the Trailways bus station to collect on that free shoe shine, including myself. However, two years later I joined the army and returned to Jacksonville from basic training at Fort Gordon, Georgia. When I walked into the bus station, I saw a man shining shoes. I walked over and sat down in one of the three chairs and placed my feet in the stirrups. The man said not a word as he shined my shoes till they glowed. After he was done, I got down from the chair and held out a dollar bill.

"Don't guess you want that free shine, Mr. Roger?" asked the man.

It took me several seconds before I recognized the gentleman. I slowly stepped down from the high bench, and he and I hugged each other.

"I would be honored to have a free shine," I told him.

My Friend Gloria

Every day, after walking the four miles from work back to my room at the boardinghouse, I would change my clothes and head down to the nearby hamburger joint for five small hamburgers for fifty cents. I would then go back to my room, lock the door, eat my burgers, and wait to fall asleep. This particular night was not going to be much different, but it was a Friday, and on Fridays I would get paid for my week's work. So before I headed up to my room to change, I cashed my check.

When I got to the boardinghouse, even before I reached the second floor I could hear a ruckus coming from the upstairs hallway. When I reached the landing, I saw three or four sailors hanging out in the hall, drinking beer, laughing, and talking really loud. I kept my eyes down and went into my room. I heard the door to the room next to mine open and close, and then I could hear them through the wall, getting louder and louder. I heard a girl squeal, and that was followed by laughter.

I changed my clothes quickly and headed back out. One of the sailors popped his head out of the room next door and asked, "Where you headed, kid?"

"I'm going for some burgers," I replied.

"Can you pick us up some?" he asked.

I shrugged. "Sure."

He gave me four dollars and told me to bring back twenty burgers. When I returned, I gave them their food and took mine to my room. During the next few hours, many more people joined the party that seemed to be going on next door. For hours they continued to drink. The more they drank, the rowdier they got.

"Get that damn slut out of here," yelled one of the men.

I heard the door open and then a loud yell. Someone fell out into the hallway. After the door closed, I slowly opened mine and peeked down the hallway. There was a woman sitting on the floor, her back against the wall. I noticed that her lip was bleeding.

"Are you okay?" I asked her.

"Can you help me to my room?"

I walked out into the hallway and helped her to her

feet. She hobbled as she leaned against my shoulder. She placed her other hand on the wall, balancing us as we walked down the hallway.

"I'm in room twenty," she said.

I helped her around the corner to her room. She unlocked her door, and I helped her to her bed. She crawled up onto the bed and sprawled there, not moving a muscle. I took the key from her hand and placed it on the dresser. Then I walked down to the bathroom at the end of the hallway and got some toilet paper for her lip. "Bye," I told her, locking her door as I left.

As I returned to my room, I saw three sailors standing in the hallway, still drinking beer. A fourth was standing in the open doorway of my room. As I approached, he moved out of my way. Not one of them said a word. I entered my room, closed the door behind me, and locked it. When I sat down on my bed, I noticed that my dresser drawer was open. Quickly, I ran over to the dresser and looked inside. My heart raced when I saw that all my money was missing. I sat down on the floor, breathing hard.

"What am I going to do for food money?" I whispered.

Looking out into the hallway, I saw no one there

now. Then suddenly I heard a commotion around the hallway near room twenty. I made my way to the corner and peeked around it to see what was happening.

"Screw that slut. Let's go," said one of the sailors, as he started down the staircase.

The other two men with him just kept laughing and banging on her door.

"Open the damn door, you slut," one sailor kept yelling.

I wanted to say something to them about my money, but I was too afraid.

"Come on. Let's get out of here," said one of the sailors.

The three of them headed down the stairs and went out the front door. I stood there for the longest time, my face against the cool wall, worrying about my money and what I was going to do for food. Suddenly the door of room twenty opened, and the woman came out into the hallway. She walked to the bathroom at the far end. When she closed the door, I turned and walked back to my room. I locked my door, slumped on my bed, and started to cry.

"Are you awake?" asked a voice at my door. When I opened my door, there stood the woman from room twenty. "Thank you for helping me. My name is Gloria."

I reached up and wiped my eyes. The tears were still running down my cheeks.

"What's wrong?" she asked.

"Those sailor guys stole all my money."

"Those bastards," she growled.

"I don't know what I'm going to do for food."

"Come on," she said, as she reached out and grabbed me by the hand.

The two of us walked to her room, and she sat me down on the edge of her bed. She picked up her purse and began to rummage through it.

"Here. Take this," she said, as she held out a ten-dollar bill. "If you run short, just let me know."

"Thank you, ma'am," I said, as I stood up and took the money from her hand.

"No. Thank you for being kind to me."

She reached over and pulled me close to her. Then she wrapped her arms around me and hugged me as tightly as she could. I remember feeling her warm bra-less breasts against the side of my face. I stood there in a total state of teenage shock.

"Would you like to spend the night in my room?" she whispered.

"No ma'am," I told her, shaking my head back and forth quickly.

"Well, if you change your mind, you just come and knock on my door."

"Thank you for the food money. I will pay you back. I really will."

"I know you will," she said, and she kissed me on the forehead.

I walked out into the hallway and turned around to look at her. She smiled at me and then closed her door.

I stood for several minutes thinking about what had just happened to me. I wanted so much to knock on her door and tell her that I wanted to stay the night, but I was too nervous. Even if she did let me back in her room, I wouldn't know what to do or say. I knew about the sex thing, but I didn't have the slightest idea how to start it.

Several times I raised my hand to knock on her door. However, every time I did, my heart began to race, and I shook so badly that I could hardly stand upright. I slowly lowered my hand, turned around, and walked back to my own room.

In the next eight months, Gloria and I became very good friends. She never would take back the ten dollars I owed her. In fact, when she had male callers to her room, she would have them pay me to go to the hamburger joint and pick up food for them. She always made sure that they bought food for me, too, and gave me a great big tip.

One Friday, she told me that she was going out of town for the weekend. I never saw her again after that.

Many times during those months, I heard sailors call my friend a slut. I'm not sure if what Gloria was doing was right or wrong. That wasn't for me to say. All I knew for sure was that she was a very kind person who cared about me. She added much to the life of a very lonely teenage boy who had nothing in life to look forward to except walking to work many days in the rain and staying all alone in his boardinghouse room.

Connie-O

I was about seventeen years old and had gotten myself a job at a hospital in Georgia as an orderly. While eating lunch one day, I heard several hospital employees gossiping about a sixteen-year-old girl in the maternity ward. They were making snide comments about her situation and would occasionally break out in laughter. It distressed me that they could talk about her as if she were worthless simply because she was unmarried and pregnant.

I rose from my seat, placed my tray in the kitchen window, and made my way up to the maternity ward. I walked behind the nurse's station and began rifling through the medical charts.

"Can I help you?" asked the head nurse, as she rounded the corner.

Thinking quickly, I said, "I am looking for some information for Dr. McCall."

The nurse rolled her eyes. "If Dr. McCall wants

information on our maternity patients, he will just have to come up here himself," she said gruffly.

I looked down at the chart in my hand—the girl's chart. Her name was Miss Cornwell. I placed the chart back in the rack and said, "I'll be on my way, then."

I returned to my duties. Miss Cornwell was the topic of the day, and I was becoming very tired of hearing everyone judge her for having a baby out of wedlock. I could only imagine how they were treating her, and I decided to go see her for myself. So after the changing of shifts, I put on a white lab coat, to look more official, and made my way to the maternity ward.

"What room is Miss Cornwell in?" I matter-of-factly asked the nurse on duty.

"Across the hall," she replied, pointing me in the right direction.

The door was closed, but I went in, anyway. A very beautiful pregnant girl looked up at me, and I felt a tug on my heart.

"Who are you?" she asked.

"I'm here to check the windows," I told her, and did as I said.

"What is your name?" she asked.

"Roger," I replied. "What's yours?"

"Twila," she answered.

I'd never heard that name before, and it struck me as very special. I wanted to say more, but I didn't know what to say. I stood there awkwardly for a moment, then finally said, "You are really very pretty."

She blushed, turned away from me, and covered her head with the blanket. I took that as a sign that I should leave, and I did. The next day, I sent two flowers to her room with an anonymous note telling her that she was pretty. The following day, I heard that she had had the baby. Again she was the talk of the hospital.

I conjured up the nerve to go see her. When I walked into her room, she was holding her new baby in her arms.

"Thank you for the beautiful flowers," she said with a smile.

I pretended not to know what she was talking about. "Flowers? I didn't send any flowers."

"Roger, nobody else around here has told me that I'm pretty," she said with a great big smile on her face. "So I know it was you."

I looked down at the baby and told her that it was beautiful, too, just like her. Then a thought occurred to me, and I asked, "Twila, will you listen to the radio between seven and eight tonight?"

She looked a little puzzled but agreed. As soon as

my shift ended, I rushed over to the local radio station
and asked the deejay to play the song "Connie-O" by
the Four Seasons and to dedicate it to Twila from
Roger. The deejay said he would.

I don't know when I got the idea in my head, but
that song was going to be the prelude to my marriage
proposal. Yes, I was going to ask her to marry me. I
wanted to protect her from people who would laugh
at her and judge her harshly for being unwed with a
baby. At exactly seven o'clock, "Connie-O" played on
the radio. I imagined Twila listening to the song and
thinking about me as I was thinking about her. That's
what I did all night long.

Next day, with a bouquet of flowers in my hand, I
headed straight for her room. With as big a smile as I
could make, I pushed open the door to her room. The
room was vacant, and my heart sank.

"Where is Twila?" I shouted.

"She was discharged early this morning," the nurse
told me, with concern in her voice.

Overcome by a feeling of doom and loneliness, I
dropped the flowers and could hardly make it back
to my workstation. I never saw Twila again.

Many years later, when I married and had a daughter, I named her Twila after the young girl I had

wanted to make my wife. I know that I barely knew the girl and that a marriage between us may have been foolish, a little crazy, and maybe just a little stupid. But when I think back to Twila and my willingness to make an "honest woman" out of her, I am happy to know that I was a boy with a good heart. I think that makes doing something a little stupid okay sometimes.

A Type-AB Man

"**I**s there any way I can get a cup of coffee with sugar?" asked the homeless man who was sitting in the hospital waiting room.

Still half asleep when I arrived for work at the hospital, I waved my hand as if to tell him to not bother me.

Entering the emergency room, I noticed Dr. McCall darting behind one of the many drawn blue curtains. Several nurses followed him closely.

"What's the deal?" I asked the nurse who was sitting at the nurses' station.

"Car accident victim, I think," she replied, without looking up from the magazine she was reading.

I walked over to the curtain and slowly peeked inside.

That's bad, I thought, as I saw an older woman lying on an ambulance gurney, her right leg bent awkwardly.

"Kiser, you wait out front and watch for Mr. Champney [the accident victim's husband]," said the head nurse, pointing her finger toward the front of the hospital. "He's flying in from Atlanta and should be here in about thirty minutes."

Walking toward the entrance, I once again had to venture through the emergency waiting room.

"Is there any way I can get a cup of coffee with lots of sugar?" asked the dingy fellow again.

Walking into the hospital gift shop, I poured a cup of hot coffee and dumped in a ton of sugar. Waiting for Mr. Champney to arrive, I watched though the large glass window as I walked back to the waiting room and handed the coffee to the man.

His name was Jeffrey; he visited the hospital emergency room several times a week with one ailment or another. The week before, he'd had a rectal itching problem, so he was given a four-pack of suppositories. Several hours later he returned and told us that his problem had not been relieved. When the nurse asked him if he had used one of the suppositories, he replied, "I used two of 'em, but they sure tasted waxy."

It took everything Dr. McCall could do to keep from laughing.

I stood outside for more than an hour waiting for Mr. Champney to arrive. Suddenly a black Cadillac raced into the driveway and came to a screeching halt.

A well-dressed man opened the back door of the car and headed toward me.

"Champney here! Where is my wife?" shouted the large man in a very authoritative voice.

As he pushed everyone to the side, I tried to explain that she was in the emergency room when I last saw her. As we reached the emergency room door, I carefully reached up and placed my hand on his arm.

"You wait here, and I'll see what's happening," I said. "No one is allowed inside except hospital personnel."

Champney would have none of that, however, and pushed me into the wall.

"Hey!" I yelled. "You can't go in there."

The gentleman stopped, gave me a very stern look, and pointed his finger at my nose.

Backing away from his large finger in my face, I pointed to the seating area and said, "You sit down over there, and I'll see where your wife is so you can see her."

The man turned slowly and began walking away.

"Jesus Christ, you stink like hell," he exclaimed at Jeffrey, as he quickly moved away.

Jeffrey smiled, reached into his shirt pocket, pulled out the two remaining suppositories, and said to the man, "Would you like a candy?"

I smiled and walk into the emergency room.

Several minutes later, I walked back to the waiting room and began to explain to Mr. Champney that the doctor was having a very difficult time finding blood. His wife had a very unusual blood type.

"I know, she has an AB blood type. Don't you fellows have any?" he asked, shaking his hands furiously in front of him.

"Excuse me," said Jeffrey, as he interrupted our conversation.

"Will you shut up?" barked Champney.

Slowly closing his mouth and looking down at the floor, Jeffrey moved backward and took his seat in the corner of the room.

The next thing I knew, Dr. McCall's hand was resting on my shoulder.

"Roger, let me have a minute here," he told me.

I walked several paces away and stopped. He explained to Mr. Champney that his wife was in need of blood and that none was available. The nearest AB blood he was able to locate was in Jacksonville, Florida, and it would take several hours for it to arrive.

"Can I have some more coffee with sugar?" Jeffrey asked me.

I walked over, took his cup, and had turned to walk away when he mumbled, "I'm type AB."

I winked at him jokingly, then walked away to get his coffee.

Upon returning, I saw Mr. Champney bent over with his head and his arms resting on the water fountain. Saying not a word, I walked over to Jeffrey and handed him his coffee.

"Really, I have AB blood," he said once again.

Still saying nothing, I walked back into the emergency room and over to Dr. McCall.

"What are we going to do?" I asked him.

"Need that blood and we need it quick," he replied.

"Doc, that leg looked pretty bad when I saw it," I voiced.

"That leg is going to be okay. The surgeon is on his way. It's the blood loss that I'm concerned about."

"This may be nothing but Jeffrey says he has AB blood type."

With a strange look on his face, Dr. McCall turned and walked toward the waiting room. Within seconds he had Jeffrey by the arm and was walking him into the emergency room. The laboratory technician was summoned and performed several blood tests on Jeffrey. Sure enough, it was found that dirty, old, homeless Jeffrey had the rare blood type classified as AB.

I immediately walked back to the waiting room and told Mr. Champney the news. Dr. McCall and Jeffrey were walking out of the emergency room when Champney yelled, "I'll buy all the blood you'll sell me."

"My blood's not for sale," Jeffrey told him in a very firm voice.

Champney's eyes immediately enlarged to the size of golf balls, and he stood there speechless.

I watched as McCall and Jeffrey disappeared down the long hallway toward the ambulance section.

"You wait here, and I'll have a talk with him," I told Champney.

I walked into the gift shop, poured myself a cup of coffee, and headed down the hallway to find Dr. McCall. After searching for about ten minutes, I located both of them in the doctor's lounge. Jeffrey was in the shower, covered from head to toe with surgical soap, and Dr. McCall was scrubbing him with what appeared to be a large toilet brush.

I stood there looking at Jeffrey's dirty, skinny, naked body, his ribs almost protruding through his sides, wondering the entire time how such a body could have something almost as valuable as gold flowing through its veins.

"Are you going to let that woman die?" I asked him.

"Well, of course not."

"But you said your blood was not for sale."

"It's not," he replied.

Dr. McCall smiled at me and then patted Jeffrey on the back several times. Soap splattered everywhere.

Within the hour, the surgeon had arrived, and the woman and Jeffrey were taken into surgery.

Several hours later, Jeffrey was once again sitting in the waiting room. He and Mr. Champney were laughing and drinking coffee together.

Later that afternoon, three of us took Mrs. Champney by ambulance to the airport and put her onto a private plane. I was standing on the runway smoking a cigarette when I saw the black Cadillac drive out onto the tarmac. As the door opened, I watched as Mr. Champney and Jeffrey emerged from the vehicle. I smiled when I looked at Jeffrey. It was the first time I'd ever seen him clean and all dressed up.

"Look at me," said Jeffrey, with tears in his eyes.

"The tie looks good, Mr. Jeffrey," I said, nodding my head.

"Would you like a candy?" he asked me as he reached toward his shirt pocket.

"No thank you, sir," I said with a smile, as I watched the two of them board the plane.

Mail Call

"Okay, men, listen up! Each of you will sit down this evening and write a letter home. You will tell your family how much you love the United States Army. Is that understood?" said Sergeant O'Rouke.

"Yes, sir!" the entire platoon shouted back.

"Dismissed!" he bellowed, and the soldiers went running in every direction back to their barracks.

This was my third week of basic training. I generally stayed in the barracks when mail call was announced; I didn't run off in anticipation like the rest of the platoon. Why would I? No one was going to be sending me any goodwill wishes.

While the other men sorted through handfuls of mail and packages from home, I would sit on my bunk and shine my boots, trying not to notice the commotion. I have to admit that I was a little jealous when I saw them eating the cookies their parents had sent, but in general it did not really bother me. I didn't have anyone who would write, and that's just the way it was. There was nothing I could do about it, so I tried not to think about it.

After showering, I dressed and headed over to the post exchange while the others were writing their letters. I purchased a Coca-Cola and a package of cheese crackers and sat at one of the small tables. Just as I finished, Sergeant O'Rouke sauntered in.

"What are you doing in here, soldier?" he shouted when he saw me.

"Having a Coke, sir," I replied.

"Hit the deck and give me twenty-five!" he ordered.

I immediately hit the floor and started counting the push-ups as I completed each one.

"Why aren't you in the barracks writing to your family?" he questioned, between numbers ten and eleven.

"Eleven! I don't have a family, sir!" I replied, going down for twelve.

"I don't give a rat's tail if you have a family or not. I told you to write home."

"Fourteen! But I don't have a home, sir."

"Then where the hell did you come here from, soldier?" he questioned.

"Sixteen! I came from an orphanage, sir!"

The sergeant kicked one of my arms out from under

me, and I hit the floor. Then he put his foot in the middle of my back and pressed down as hard as he could.

"Don't you be handing me that line of bullcrap, son."

"Really, sergeant, I don't have any family. Really, I don't."

"You get your butt back over to the barracks, right now. You write me a letter, and you bring it to me. Understand?" he shouted.

"But who do I write it to?"

"I don't give a damn if you write to Santa Claus. You write a letter, and you have it to me by eighteen-hundred hours."

"Yes, sir," I said, as I got up off the floor.

I walked back to my barracks and borrowed a tablet and a pencil from one of the men in my squad. I sat down on my bunk and wrote the following letter.

Dear Santa Claus,

I am now living at Fort Gordon. I am in the army now. The army is my new home. I am learning a lot about how to win a war. I can shoot and run very fast. I am making my very own money and I am going to be a real soldier someday.

Roger Dean Kiser

I placed the letter in an envelope and sealed it. I walked over to the orderly room and asked to see the sergeant. I was advised that he was not in the office and that I should put the letter on his desk, so I placed the sealed envelope on the corner of his desk and returned to the barracks.

At nine o'clock, the lights were out and everyone was in his bunk. I rested there, thinking about how hard life was in the army. I said a prayer asking God to help me keep up with the other men as we trained. Just as I was about to fall asleep, the lights came on.

"Where is that little piece of crap?" demanded Sergeant O'Rouke, as he walked between the bunks.

I sat up in bed and watched the sergeant as he stomped down the aisle and stopped at the foot of my bunk. The other men also sat up but remained perfectly quiet.

"What is this garbage?" asked the sergeant, as he shook the letter I had written.

"It's the letter you told me to write."

"Read this letter out loud," he instructed, throwing it on the foot of my bunk.

Slowly, I picked up the letter and began to read it to him.

The men throughout the barracks began to laugh and whistle as loud as they could.

"Shut up!" yelled Sergeant O'Rouke.

The men became perfectly quiet.

"You think I'm an idiot?" asked the sergeant.

"No, sir!"

The large man reached down, grabbed my foot-locker, and turned it upside down. The contents spilled all over the floor.

"I only wrote what you told me to write," I said.

"I told you to write home!" he argued.

"No sir, Sergeant. I told you that I did not have any family, and you told me to write to Santa Claus. That's why I don't get any mail here, 'cause I don't have a home."

All the men in the barracks looked at one another. One of the men sitting on the side of his bed began to laugh.

"Santa Claus!" he said, laughing aloud.

Everyone then stared at him, and he stopped laughing.

"Clean up this mess and report to me in the morning," Sergeant O'Rouke yelled.

As the sergeant left the barracks, he turned out the light, leaving me to pack my footlocker in the dark. About a week later, I was shocked to hear my name called out for mail call.

"Kiser, Kiser, Kiser," yelled the man as he set three packages aside.

During the next three weeks of my basic training, I received seven more packages of cookies and hard candy in the mail. I never knew from whom they came. There was no return address on the packages. I could only guess that they came from families of the men in my platoon. Maybe even from Sergeant O'Rouke himself. Or Santa Claus.

The Lingering Look of Disappointment

I was finally being discharged from the U. S. Army. I'd been stationed in Alaska and was returning to Florida, my "home." This was not a happy day for me, however. I was leaving behind a kind and wonderful woman named Maggie, who was pregnant with my child. I could not get permission from the army to marry her. Being an orphan and having been told constantly that I was a bastard, I was greatly disturbed that my child would be called the same.

Here I was, one of the great protectors of this great country, in full dress uniform, with tears streaming down my face. I do not suppose that this sight instilled a lot of confidence in the Americans who were sharing my plane ride.

When I got back to Jacksonville, I had nowhere to go and no one to turn to. I had difficulty finding a good-paying job, so I got a temporary job scraping shingles off rooftops. I was earning very little, and I knew that at that rate I would never raise enough money to get back to Alaska to marry Maggie before the baby was born. This made my heart very heavy. I had already decided that I would do almost anything to stop another human being from being labeled a bastard.

One afternoon at the local coffee shop, I met two men about my age who were from Canada and were headed back that way by car. When I told them that I needed to get back to Alaska, they invited me to join them. That would certainly get me much closer than I was now, and this really lifted my spirits.

I gathered my meager belongings and the next day hopped in the car, ready to head toward Canada, but when I spied a pair of handguns lying on the passenger seat, I was ready to hop back out. I asked about them.

"Oh, those?" said Bill, the driver. "They aren't real. They're just starter pistols."

I chose to believe him because I had my mind set on Canada. He put the guns in the glove compartment as the other passenger got in, and the three of us were on our way.

"How much money you got?" asked Bill, once we were on the road.

"I have twenty dollars," I replied.

"That's not going to get us very far," said the other guy.

"Don't you have any money?" I asked, a bit confused, because how did they plan to drive all the way to Canada without any money?

It turned out that they didn't have any money, and I got the feeling that I'd been asked to come along just to fund their trip. We decided that we would go as far as the twenty dollars would take us and then figure out something else.

As we were passing through the little town of Dinsmore, I reminisced out loud about a girl from the area that I used to date. Her father owned a small country market. "Why don't we stop so I can say hello?" I suggested.

When we arrived at the store, Bill reached into the glove compartment and took out the guns. He handed one to his friend.

My eyes widened. "What are you going to do?" I asked.

"Get some damn money! What do you think?" Bill said.

I backed up. "I really don't want any part of this!"

"Then get your bastard ass down the road," said his friend.

I don't know why I didn't leave right then and there, and maybe I'll never know. Maybe it was because he called me a bastard. That one word always did hurt me to the core. Maybe I thought that I had no other choice.

We walked into the old man's world, and I will never forget him looking at me with those sad eyes, shaking his head when he saw the guns.

"Roger, what are you doing, young man?" he asked. "You're a good boy. Why are you doing this?"

"I'm sorry, Mr. Feister," I said, looking down at the floor.

Bill walked up to him, put his gun right in Mr. Feister's face, and ordered him to put all his money into a paper bag. The old man filled the bag and handed it to Bill's friend. Then Bill pushed Mr. Feister hard against the wall, and the poor old man fell down and hit his head.

Some smarts came to me suddenly, and I ran as fast as I could toward Bill, shoving him through the screen door and knocking him onto the porch outside.

"You damn son of a bitch!" I yelled.

Half inside and half outside the store, I heard Mr. Feister get to his feet. He said sadly, "All you had to do was ask me, son. I would have helped you."

"What the hell are you doing?!" shouted Bill's friend.

It hadn't occurred to me that one of them would try to shoot. We were all just scared kids, really. I shouted, "Shut up!"

I was scared and ashamed, but it was too late to back out now. I was in too deep. I moved quickly toward Bill's friend and snatched the money-filled sack from his hand and dumped the contents on the counter. I quickly divided it into two equal piles—about thirty dollars each. I gave an apologetic look, along with half the money, to Mr. Feister.

Bill was standing at the door looking pretty frightened—my rage was so great. I pitched a penny at his head and stormed past him through the door without looking back at Mr. Feister. We drove about 100 miles without saying a word. The deplorable incident was never mentioned. Within three months, I was free of Bill and his friend, and I had somehow managed to make it to Alaska without breaking any more laws.

I married Maggie in January, just a matter of days before our wonderful son, James Brian, was born. About two hours after the wedding ceremony and before James was born, the FBI knocked on my front door. They handcuffed me and took me away. I was sentenced to five years, which was suspended, and then was given five years of probation. I suppose the judge was lenient because I had given back half the money. Maybe Mr. Feister had put in a good word for me.

After many years, I came to accept and come to terms with what I had done that day, but I still haven't gotten over the look of disappointment that I saw in Mr. Feister's eyes. I have endeavored all my life never to see that look again directed at me, and for that I thank Mr. Feister.

Tears in Prison

"**W**hat the hell are you looking at?" shouted the large man at the urinal beside mine.

I couldn't help but notice that he was crying, and maybe I had let my eyes linger too long on his face. "Just minding my own business," I said, quickly turning my head to face the wall.

I was surprised to see such a large, mean-looking man with tears in his eyes. I mean, this was a prison—the Big House. Everyone knew that tears were a sign of weakness, and almost everyone preyed upon weakness. That was the unspoken rule.

"What was it you were looking at?" he asked again, zipping up his pants. When I didn't respond, he grabbed me by the shoulders.

"Nothing!" I said, jerking away from him.

As I zipped up my pants, he wiped his eyes with his calloused hand.

"It's hard here. It's real hard," he said.

"I've only been here for two days," I replied. (It was two days of a one-year sentence for purchasing beer for underage kids, but after two escapes, I would end up serving three years and six months.)

"My family came today. It was the first time I have seen my kids in almost two years. First time my kids ever seen me in prison clothes," he told me.

"I don't have to worry about that. I don't have any family," I said. My wife, Maggie, had made it clear that she had no interest in knowing me anymore, so it was the sad truth. I really had no one—again.

"Everyone has to have a family."

He placed his foot up on urinal.

"Not everyone," I said, as I moved away from the urinal.

"No mother or father?"

"Never knew either one of them. Raised in an orphanage," I replied.

"Then it shouldn't be too hard on you here."

"That's right," I said. "These places are just like being home to me. Orphanage, juvenile hall, jail, or prison, they are all the same."

"Frank," he said, holding out his hand.

"Roger," I said back, reaching out to shake his hand.

"Kind of makes me wish that I would have taken a different road," he said with somewhat of a laugh.

"What you in for?" I asked.

"Interstate transportation of a stolen motor vehicle."

"How much time you get?" I asked.

"Seven years," he responded.

"How much time you got left?"

"Got three under my belt, less my good time; I figure I'll be out of here in another two years."

We stood in the doorway of the bathroom talking and watching for the guard to make his rounds. Frank talked about his two children and how he thought that he had let them down. I watched as once in a while, tears welled up in his eyes.

"If there's one thing that this place has, it's plenty of loneliness," he said, wiping his eyes again.

I found it so strange to see such a large man, with muscles like that of bodybuilder Charles Atlas, standing before me with tears rolling down his cheeks. Finally, we decided that we had better head back to our bunks before the guards came around.

Once again I held out my hand. He reached out, took my hand, and squeezed it. Then, for just a split second, he rested his head on my shoulder.

"You don't know who I am, do you." It wasn't a question.

"No, sir. I don't."

"What you saw here tonight stays here. You got it?" he ordered.

"Yes, sir."

"You'll never have a problem for as long as you are here," he said.

After that night, we never spoke again. We would nod our heads when we passed in the prison yard. I never did know exactly who he was. However, I knew he was basically a good man who had a kind heart and loved his children.

I had always heard that the best way to get along in prison was to mind one's own business. You were to see nothing, you were to hear nothing, and if asked, you were to know nothing. However, I saw things and I knew things—and often, what I saw and what I knew touched me deeply and kept me going.

The Jail Bird

"Yard will be closed in thirty minutes," came the voice from the loudspeakers that hung on the quarter-mile wall of the prison. My duties as x-ray technician at the prison hospital were completed for the day. I headed down the long steel corridor, looking for my friend Wendall.

Wendall and I were from different states. Even though I was a state prisoner, both of us were incarcerated at a federal penitentiary in California. Wendall's crime was stealing a car. Mine was for purchasing a six-pack of beer for a party attended by underage kids, for which I'd received a one-year sentence.

I shouted when I saw Wendall coming out of the library.

"Let's hit the yard and get some air for a while," he said, walking my way.

We approached the two open steel doors, turned left, and walked out into the yard. Off in the distance, I could see the two twenty-foot chain-link fences with circular barbed razor wire that surrounded the large prison. Between the two fences, the ground had been sprayed with a white powder. Anyone who tried to escape and who made it across the first fence would leave a trail of white footprints.

Several hundred yards to my right and to my left were two guard towers. Each stretched forty to fifty feet into the air. They were round with a glass-type house sitting on top of massive concrete pillars. Guards sat atop with automatic weapons to watch for escapes or any sort of major disturbance in the yard.

The yard was filled with about 600 inmates, each group self-segregated into a section: the whites in one area, the blacks in another, and the Mexicans in their own section. In addition to these groups, there were the gangs. Anyone who moved around the yard would do so at a reasonable distance from the gangs. Even accidentally bumping into someone in the yard would be looked upon as an insult. Such an incident could get you beaten, shanked, or even raped.

Carefully, we walked out to an open area, sat down on the ground, and began to talk. As we talked, we watched the weight lifters in the weight area. Several groups were throwing a baseball back and forth. Others were pitching a rubber ball against a cement wall as though they were playing handball. Some prisoners were running around the track, trying to stay in shape.

When you are a prisoner in the yard, you always keep your eyes open and stay alert. You never allow anyone to walk up behind you. If someone walks up behind you, you immediately stand up and face him down.

Although there are hundreds of different conversations taking place, you are not allowed to eavesdrop. Even if you overhear the conversation, you had better not act or look as though you'd heard anything. Even looking in the direction of a conversation might start a serious confrontation.

As we talked, we noticed a large group of men gathering at the cement wall. Within a minute, almost everyone on the yard was walking in that direction. As Wendall and I stood up, I noticed the guards in the towers walk out onto the cement ramp, each with his rifle in his hand.

Within a minute or so, word had spread throughout the yard that a bird had flown into the cement wall and injured itself. We slowly made our way over to the wall. Sure enough, there was a bird lying on the ground with an injured wing. One of the musclebound weight lifters reached down, picked up the bird, and began to stroke its head. The prisoners packed in tightly to see what was happening.

As I stood there, I looked back and forth at the face of every prisoner. Something had changed, even if only for a moment. No one was on guard, and no one was worried about being hurt. All that seemed to matter was the injured bird.

"Disperse and return to your stations," sounded the loudspeaker.

Slowly the crowd started to move apart. I watched as the captain walked across the yard, swinging a billy club in his hand. As he reached the wall, he pushed the club into the chest of the weight lifter and ordered him to put the injured bird down. The large man carefully placed the bird on the ground and then just stood there. The captain raised his club and struck the bird on the head. The bird fluttered its wings and flew around in a small circle for several seconds. Then it lay lifeless on the ground. Suddenly a cry of protest came from the entire crowd—a sound that I had never heard before. They were not sounds of madness, but cries of pain and sorrow.

Again, I watched the faces of these hardened men as they cried out in protest. I watched as several of them covered their faces and sat down on the ground.

The guards in the towers loaded and raised their rifles. Gradually, the yard started to empty.

That night was not like other nights in the prison. There was no laughing or talking between the cells. All was silent. I sat in my cell thinking about what I had seen that day. I wondered why such a thing would be so dramatic to these men. I wondered how many of these men had been struck, beaten, or knocked to the ground when they were helpless, defenseless children.

That event seemed to be an unusual thing when I was in prison. Almost any crime would be accepted or tolerated. Anything goes, except hurting a child or a defenseless animal. I wonder what it was that I saw in their faces that day. I wonder what it was that made these hardened men open their hearts for that moment.

I never said anything to anyone about the bird. I do not think it was ever mentioned again. The next day all was back to normal. Everyone was once again on guard and watching his back. However, I do know this: I learned a very good lesson that day. I saw that no matter how hard and mean a man is, there is something somewhere that can touch the inside of his heart.

The Bible Pages

I t was Sunday morning, and I began to worry when my friend Wendall did not show up at E-block. The night before, we had gone to the theater to see the movie *Born Free*. It was strange how a movie about lions could have such an impact on me. It was amazing to me that a human being could identify his situation with that of three lion cubs.

I do not think that it was the "being free" part that mattered to me. I had never been free. I had spent all those terrible years in the orphanage, never having the right to speak unless spoken to. I had never had the right to get a drink of water or use the bathroom without asking permission. The freedom part thus meant very little to me. I guess it was the fact that the lion cubs had to survive against all odds that made me start tearing up during the movie.

Just as I was about to head out of the cell block, Wendall walked in.

"Damn good movie last night," he said as he approached me.

"Yeah, still a little numb here. Not sure why, though," I told him.

We headed to the library, which was about halfway down the quarter-mile steel corridor. Hundreds of prisoners marched past us, going here and there, and their voices were echoing off the steel walls as they talked. In the distance I could hear the slamming of cell doors as the prisoners were being released for yard time.

When we arrived, I opened the door for Wendall to enter the library. I walked in behind him and saw that there were about twenty inmates sitting in the small room. Many were studying for their general equivalency diploma, and others were reading for pleasure.

An hour of free time to get one's mind off the present-day situation, I thought, looking about the room.

"What's your pleasure?" asked Wendall. He pointed to a far wall that was full of books.

"Not for me," I told him. "Hell, I ain't read a book since the sixth grade. I'm just here for the company."

Just then, the library door opened and Wendall's eyes became huge. I turned around and looked toward the door. Standing in the doorway were three Mexican gang members, one of whom was seriously big. Three or four men got up from their seats and moved against the wall, waiting for a chance to leave the room. One of the gang members motioned his head, and the other two moved out of the way, clearing the doorway. The four men walked rather quickly out the door and began running down the corridor.

"Is there a Bible in here?" asked the large Mexican inmate.

No one said a word.

The three of them walked over to the wall of books and began dumping them off the shelf onto the floor. The commotion stopped when one of the men held up a Bible. The leader took it and sat down at a wooden table near the doorway. He reached into his shirt pocket and took out what appeared to be a pouch of tobacco. He opened the Bible and tore out a page. Then he began rolling the tobacco into a cigarette, using the Bible page as a cigarette paper.

Several of the men registered their displeasure over this treatment of the Bible by grumbling and standing up. I was surprised that they cared.

"You got a problem?" asked the Mexican man, pointing his finger at each of them.

"That ain't right, and you know it," said one of the men.

The gang member, never taking his eyes off the men, reached over and tore out several more pages from the Bible. The room remained quiet for several minutes, without anyone making a move or a sound.

I looked over at Wendall and he looked at me. Suddenly he slid back his chair, and he too stood up. I sat there wondering what was about to happen. Then several more men stood up. With my heart beating ninety miles per hour, I also stood up. One of the men at the far back table walked over to the where the three men were sitting. He reached down and picked up the Bible, along with the three or four torn-out pages. He stuck the pages back into the book, then slowly walked over to the bookshelf and placed the Bible onto the shelf. He returned to his seat, sat down, and began to read to himself.

The room remained very silent. Almost everyone in the room was staring at the three men. No one's eyes moved from them. I watched as the larger man looked at his two friends. He gently motioned his head to one side. The three of them got up from the table, and they walked out of the room.

By the next morning, news of the incident had

spread throughout the entire prison. I am not sure how the word came down, but it was put out to the entire prison population: defacing a Bible or a religious pamphlet was in the category of children and defenseless animals. It was something you just didn't mess with.

I'd never figured that anyone in prison could be principled like that—would care enough to stand up for something he believed in. I thought it was just about being tough and not getting preyed upon. I was mistaken—and gladly so.

A Life Preserver

"*It's hard for me to learn. There's something wrong with me inside my head. That's what they tell me at the orphanage,*" I told Mrs. Dryer, the school principal.

Mrs. Dryer just shook her head and said, "Roger, can you do me a favor?"

"Yes, ma'am," I replied.

"One day, you are going to be free of that home. One day, you will be somebody special. There is a special goodness about you that sets you apart from the rest of the class. I am not quite sure what it is, but it is a special quality that you possess. You always seem to bounce back, no matter what they do to you at the orphanage. Someday when you are all grown up, special and free, will you remember I told you that?" she asked.

"Yes, ma'am. I won't forget what you told me," I replied.

Over the course of twenty-three years, I'd made my way from the orphanage to the reform school to jail to the army and then, finally, to prison—a successful career by the system's standards. When I was released from prison, it was the first time that I was free of the system—free for the first time in my life to make choices for myself.

I stood outside the prison, not having the slightest idea who I was as a person. I did not know how to do anything for myself. I was wearing a baggy suit that the prison had given me. I had less than fifty dollars in my pocket. I had nowhere to go and no one to turn to. I stood there searching my mind for something that would help me to take my next step. I looked up into the cloudy sky and closed my eyes.

Mrs. Dryer's words from long ago rang in my ears.

I opened my eyes and said aloud, "I remember, Mrs. Dryer, I remember."

Her kind and sincere words were mine and mine alone. For much of my life, I possessed nothing, and what little I did have was taken away, but those words and the meaning behind them could not be taken away from me. I had no idea at the time that Mrs. Dryer had done so much for me. She knew about the daily beatings and the other abuse I suffered as a boy. She knew that it was just a matter of time before my ship would wreck and sink and that when it did, I would be left treading water all by myself.

So there I was, outside the prison, treading water all

by myself. How wonderful that I just now understood that Mrs. Dryer had tossed me a life preserver so many years ago, and I'd finally caught it. I was ready to make a life for myself, and I did. Since the day of my release, I've been an outstanding citizen—thanks, in part, to Mrs. Dryer.

The Little White Box

"What is it that Mrs. Mathers keeps talking on about?" I asked the nurse at the front desk of the nursing home where I had been employed for about a week.

"I don't know. I just do not know." Mrs. Mathers had been in the nursing home for two weeks. Her family figured that she wouldn't live another month and so chose to place her in a nursing home. The whole time, she'd gone on about some damn little white plastic box.

"Something about a box?" I questioned.

"Just get her dressed for bed and forget about her ramblings," she instructed.

"Yes ma'am," I said, and I walked away from the nursing station.

Every day when I came to work, Mrs. Mathers asked about the little white box. She stretched out in her bed all day with her hands partially covering her face. Each time I moved her hands away from her face to wash them, I could see tears rolling down her cheeks.

"Before I die, my little white box, please," she'd say.

"Mrs. Mathers, I don't know what you mean," I told her.

Every day it was the same routine. No matter what I said to her, I couldn't understand what she was taking about.

Several times in the next week, the doctor was called to attend to Mrs. Mathers. Each time, I stood outside her room to see if the doctor would pull her through, and each time, after the doctor left, I would go in and wipe her forehead to make sure she was comfortable.

"My house. My little white box. Please," she said over and over.

At 3:30 PM, as I was about to get off work, I walked up to the desk and pulled out Mrs. Mathers's chart.

I read that 1333 Whitmark was her last known address. I drove the five miles or so till I located the house. I arrived to see that there was an estate sale going on. There were cars and people everywhere.

"You're going to have to get a number if you are going to bid," said one of the men, as I walked up.

"I'm not going to bid."

I walked around the house for about ten minutes, looking at everything that was tagged for sale. As I entered the dining room, I saw a gentleman wrapping various items and stuffing them into cardboard boxes. Sitting on the edge of the table was a little white plastic box.

"Excuse me. By any chance, did you buy this little white box?" I asked.

"I bought everything in this room," he stated.

"Could I look inside this little white box?"

"Sure. There's nothing in there of any value," he replied.

I slowly opened the box and peeked inside.

Oh, my God, I thought.

"Can I have this box?" I asked immediately, trying not to betray my surprise.

"Not worth nothing to me," he answered.

I ran out of the house as fast as I could, headed back to the nursing home, and rushed into Mrs. Mathers's room.

"Mrs. Mathers, it's me, Roger. Look what I've got," I said excitedly.

She opened her eyes slowly and began to shake as she reached out and took the little white box from my hand.

"Water," she said.

I walked over to the sink, got her a cup of water, set it down on the dinner tray, and stood there watching.

"Thank you, dear."

"You're very welcome," I told her, as I patted her on the hand.

I wanted her to know that I understood that she was a fine woman and a private person. I nodded as I left her room with my most courteous manners.

When I returned to work the next day, I learned that Mrs. Mathers had passed away during the night. In all my years of working in nursing homes, there were many deaths, but I attended only two funerals. Mrs. Mathers was one of them.

I stood by the casket for more than an hour as many people filed past. I could not count the times I heard her friends say, "Jane looks at least twenty years younger with her dentures in."

I Accept This Award with Much Honor, My Lady

Heading down the Alaska (or Alcan) Highway into Canada was quite an adventure. It seemed like a never-ending road made entirely of rocks: little rocks, big rocks, hard rocks, soft rocks, red rocks, white rocks, black rocks. Every kind and type of rock known to humanity was used to make that ungodly road.

The worst thing about those darn rocks was that they constantly hit the bottom of every vehicle that drove over it. They never stopped hitting the bottom of the car as long as it was moving, and in time it would drive a person insane. I am talking about hour upon hour of rocks clinging, clanging, pinging, and banging. My head, my ears, and my mind could finally take no more of the loud noise beating against the bottom of the car. So my companion, a fellow who was traveling with me, and I decided that we would pull off the road at the next available place to rest.

I had no idea where we were as I looked at the map, and I really didn't care. All I knew for sure was that Alaska was miles behind us and that we were now traveling south, somewhere in the Yukon Territory of Canada, heading toward the lower forty-eight states.

I was twenty-four years old and had been released from prison about two months ago. I had returned to Alaska to see if anything could be worked out among my ex-wife, my two sons, and me. I was willing to do anything to keep the family together for the sake of my two boys. However, my ex-wife had already started a new life for herself, and she told me so by flipping me her middle finger. It was clear that I should head down the road and never come back.

That's exactly what I did. It really didn't matter to anyone on the face of the Earth where I came from, where I went, or what I did. Because I had been raised in an orphanage for most of my life and had had no family, it made little difference to me or anyone else whether I moved right or left, forward or backward, or up or down .

The snow was piled twenty feet high on each side of the road, and off in the distance I could see a sign. As we approached it, we saw that it said BURWASH LODGE, 1 MILE. That was a glorious sight to me, because I knew that it meant there would be hot coffee and hot food, but more than that, it would give us several hours of rest and some much-needed quiet from the banging rocks.

We pulled up to the lodge, parked, and walked into the lobby. I immediately noticed that there were eight or nine young girls working at the lodge. I walked into the restaurant, sat down at one of the tables in a far corner, and ordered a cup of hot coffee. I had with me several small bundles of legal papers, which I had promised to complete for some friends. (After the first year of my prison sentence, I had often spent time in the legal library, which is where I learned to prepare writs.)

"Would you like more coffee?" the waitress asked in a soft voice.

As I looked up, I saw one of the most beautiful girls I have ever seen on the face of the Earth. Even to this day, that evaluation is still very true. I picked up my coffee cup and held it toward her so she could fill it.

"Thank you very much," I said, as I smiled back at her.

I had not dated or had any contact with a woman whatsoever in almost four years. My ex-wife had never visited me in prison. I could not believe my own behavior now, but I was not looking the waitress up and down as she walked away. That aspect appeared to be so unimportant to me, for some reason. I was just taken by the beauty of her face and the kindness that I could see in her eyes; when she came near me, I felt a calmness I had never known.

During the next few hours, I worked on my legal petitions and finally managed to complete them. As I was about to get up and walk outside to smoke a cigarette, the beautiful waitress came walking back over to my table with the coffeepot. I placed my hand over the top of my coffee cup and told her that I did not want anything more to drink. Then we began to talk. I told her that my name was Roger and that I was from Florida, which was located in the United States. She made it clear to me that she was very aware of where Florida was.

She held out her hand, which I shook, and she said, "My name is Anne, and I am very glad to meet you, Roger."

For as long as I live, I will never forget taking her beautiful hand in mine. The feeling that came over me can barely be described in words: the warmth, the tenderness, the joy, and the happiness that I felt at that very moment. An inner peace came over me; it was something that I had never felt, as a boy or a man.

Anne and I walked around for hours and hours just

talking. I looked at her beautiful face and could hardly believe that such a lovely woman would even talk to someone like me, much less like me or think that what I had to say was important or meaningful. If ever there was a time in my life when I started to feel like an equal person, to feel good about myself, to build character, or to become a real human being who believed that he was worth something, it was then. My meeting this wonderful young woman did all of that, from the very first moment.

It was getting late, and I knew that it was about time to head back out onto the road. I located the friend who was giving me a ride to the States and told him I was ready to go. He said he was talking with a girl named Monica, who was a college student from British Columbia. I told him about Anne and said that I had never met anyone so beautiful and kind.

"There are a lot of fish in the sea," he said, as we walked out and got into his car.

"Not like her," I said.

I turned around and saw Anne standing on the porch with her coat wrapped around her.

"Do you want to stay here?" the man asked.

"Could we stay just for supper and then leave?"

We got out of the car and walked back toward the

lodge. Anne stuck out her hand and I grabbed it tightly. I almost felt like crying, but I believed that a man could not do that in front of a woman. Anne told me that she was off work for the remainder of the day, so I asked her to have dinner with me.

I ate as slowly as I could, hoping that the time I had left with Anne would last as long as possible. I looked up and saw my traveling companion motioning to me. I excused myself and walked over to him.

"It's too damn late to really get back on the road tonight, so we might as well get a room and stay until morning," he suggested.

My heart just about jumped out of my chest. I was so happy and excited. I walked back over to the table where Anne was sitting and sat down. I was a little hesitant to tell her we were staying the night, because I did not want her to think that I was staying because of any sexual thoughts about her. Besides, I looked at myself in the mirror every morning. I well knew that no such thing could ever happen between a beautiful woman like Anne and me. So I did not even think about it.

I watched my friend walk out into the lobby. He returned several minutes later, telling me the number of the room we would be staying in. Anne and I sat for two or three more hours, just talking and laughing with each other. I have never enjoyed the company of a woman so much. At about midnight, we got up from the table, said good night to each other, and walked up the stairs together to go to our rooms. I turned and looked into Anne's eyes and still could not believe how beautiful she was. I squeezed her hand as tightly as I could, and then she moved her face toward mine, and we kissed for the first time.

"Would you like to come to my room?" she asked me.

I was so scared that I did not know what to say. Anne took me by my hand and very gently led me into her room. We talked for another hour or so, and all of a sudden the most wonderful, warm, and kind feeling came over me. I was no longer scared. I stood up and walked very slowly over to the most beautiful woman I had ever known, took her by the hands, and gently pulled her up from the chair onto her feet. I wrapped my arms around her, kissed her gently on the lips, and looked into her eyes. That was the first time in my life that I had ever seen that kind of love for me in another human being's face.

It is a night I will remember for the rest of my life. There was no good or bad, right or wrong, handsome or ugly, short or tall, thin or fat. There were none of those kinds of things that night—just wonderful goodness and kindness, and the warmth that a man and a woman should really feel for each other when their hearts are looking to be needed by someone special.

Anne and I left the lodge several days later, and within a year we were married. We had a beautiful daughter, whom we named Twila Anne. Twila has now grown up and owns her own dance studio in Canada. Anne and I separated when Twila was only about two years old. I couldn't get over the horrors of what the orphanage had done to me as a child. I couldn't get it through my thick head that a beautiful young woman who was also wonderful, kind, and intelligent could ever fall in love with someone like me.

If I accomplish nothing else in my lifetime, there is one thing I can very proudly say: "It was an honor to have been kissed by one of the most beautiful women I have ever known."

Betty Boo

Anne and I rented a car in Canada and were heading south toward Florida to get married.

As we were traveling through Montana, several unmarked police cars stopped us and began to search through our things. They told us that they were searching for guns. I found that rather hard to believe, because they were going through all my legal documents and reading my personal letters. I mean, how many handguns can a person stuff inside a letter-size envelope?

About the time they were going to allow us to continue on our trip, one of the officers noticed that I was an American and that Anne was a Canadian. We were immediately arrested and taken to the jailhouse in Great Falls, Montana. They questioned us for hours.

When we were released, I was advised that I could leave and continue on my journey. I asked about Anne and was told that she would be taken back to

Canada in several hours and handed over to the authorities. I thought I would die right then and there. There was no way that I was going to leave Anne behind, no matter what I had to do. I would have done anything to get her back, and I really mean *anything*, no matter how bad or illegal it might have been.

I followed the police car to the Canadian border at Sweetgrass, Montana, where they allowed me to kiss Anne before they took her away. I told her that I loved her more than anything in the world and would do whatever it took to get us back together. I told her to get a room at the hotel on the Canadian side and call me at the pay phone at the border station as soon as she was settled. The next two days, I talked with Anne on the phone every waking moment. I told her that I was trying to arrange a marriage ceremony that would take place at the border crossing.

The next day, I found out from the state authorities that this could not be arranged and that there was no one who could legally help me. I decided right then to take matters into my own hands. I could not get it through my head why a man and a woman who lived on the same planet and loved one another could not be together. Some idiot in the past had drawn invisible lines on the face of the Earth and had told people that they must stop right here, on this spot, and not take another step—that for some unknown reason, they were different and were not allowed across a line drawn in the sand. That was so ridiculous to me. I did not care what the Americans said, and I did not care what the Canadians said. I was going to get Anne at any cost.

I noticed that in the evenings there was only one guard on the Canadian side and that the U.S. guard went home. As I stood there late one evening looking across at the Canadian side, a very nice-looking girl came up and asked if I was looking for a date. I told her that I was, but it would be with the girl I was going to marry. I remembered seeing this same girl talking with the Canadian and U.S. guards the day before.

When she realized that she was wasting her time she said, "Good-bye." Then she walked away.

"Hey, wait a minute," I yelled at her.

She turned around and said, "Well, big boy, that was a fast change of heart."

"No, that is not what I want," I told her.

I asked her how well she knew the Canadian guard who was working the Coutts, Alberta, guard crossing.

She told me that he was a nice person, but that he was always trying to get her to give him free favors. I explained my situation and asked her what she would charge me to get him out of the small building, just long enough for me to get Anne across to the U.S. side of the border. She told me that it would cost me fifty dollars. I told her that I would give her twenty-five now and the other twenty-five after I got Anne across.

I watched as she talked, laughed, and joked with the Canadian guard for more than an hour. She finally turned him around, and with his back toward me, I ran across the border toward the small hotel where Anne was staying. When I knocked on her motel room door, she opened it and her eyes became big and pretty. I could tell that she was surprised to see me. She smiled and kissed me as hard as she could. It was so wonderful to feel her arms around me.

I told her to grab her things as fast as she could, that we had to hurry and get across the border. When we got back to the border crossing, the guard was nowhere to be seen. Anne and I ran to my motel, gathered my things, and packed them into the car. Then Anne went back up to the room to use the bathroom. As I turned around, I saw the girl standing there with a strange look on her face.

"Going to skip out on me?" she said.

"I would not do that."

I reached in my pocket, counted out twenty-five dollars, and handed it to her. She took the money and then reached into her purse and took out the other twenty-five dollars I had given her. She placed all the bills together, rolled them up, and handed them back to me.

"What is this?" I asked.

"Just wanted to make sure that you were not a liar," she said.

She turned around and walked away. After traveling about twenty feet, she stopped, turned back around, and said, "By any chance, do you have a brother?"

"I don't have anybody," I said.

"They call me Betty Boo, and I don't have anybody, either," she said rather softly.

She lowered her eyes toward the ground, smiled faintly at me, and turned back around. I saw her wipe her eyes on a dirty tissue as she slowly shuffled away into the evening.

Goodbye, Mrs. Usher

I was living in California when I received a telephone call informing me that Mrs. Usher, the kind woman who took me out of the juvenile shelter and welcomed me to her home for Thanksgiving dinner, had died. I had never felt such despair for the loss of someone. The kindness and love she showed me as a child had meant the world to me, and I've always credited her with helping to shape me into the kind person I am today. If it hadn't been for her, I might never have straightened out my screwed-up life as much as I did.

I wanted to pay her my respects, since she was one of the very few people in my young life who had treated me kindly. The next day I flew from California to Florida to attend the funeral. Knowing how important Mrs. Usher and I were to each other, her children graciously paid for my flight; otherwise, I would not have been able to go.

When I arrived in Florida, several members of the

family met me at the airport. I didn't know most of them very well, if at all, and others were total strangers. I did not know what to say or what to do. Once again finding myself in an awkward situation, I kept my mouth shut and remained perfectly quiet. When everyone moved to the right, I moved to the right. When everyone moved to the left, I followed. It appeared that things had not changed much with me in the last thirty years.

We arrived at the house from my past. It felt strange that this wonderful, kind woman was nowhere to be found and would never be seen or heard in that house again. I walked slowly into the house and immediately noticed the smell of cooked eggs from breakfast that morning—the same eggs that the Ushers purchased on Wednesdays, and only at the Winn Dixie store, because they were a dime cheaper.

I did not know how to feel when someone I cared about died. What was I supposed to do, and what was I supposed to be feeling? I really did not feel much of anything at all, except numbness and sadness. I had never known anyone who died who had been a part of my life. Orphans do not know the feeling of the loss of someone who cared about them and maybe even loved them. We don't know about those things.

I do know this for a fact, however: orphans don't do dying very well, and it's rather embarrassing when you don't know how to feel inside.

The day of the funeral was hard for me, and I guess it was for everyone else, too. People were crying and grieving. I just stood around quietly, watching all the people. I took note of how they all acted, just in case someone else I cared about died. Then I would have some idea of what to do, how to look, and how to act.

There were hundreds, if not thousands, of flowers on the beautiful casket. I kept trying not to think about the wonderful, kind, and loving woman who was lying inside that box. I knew that she would be in a hole covered up with dirt and that I would never see her again.

I kept saying to myself, over and over, *I love you, Mrs. Usher. I love you, Mrs. Usher*, so that she might hear me in my mind.

The entire time this was happening, I stood there like a dummy. I was really embarrassed because I did not know where to sit when the funeral finally started. I was not part of her family, but I was not just a distant acquaintance, either. That's how it is when you're an orphan. You're always (sort of) stuck in between, and people are shifting you back and forth, trying to make you feel comfortable. So you just smile at them, look sad, and hope that no one notices that you really don't fit in.

All of a sudden it was over, thank God, and everyone started walking around the cemetery. They were all talking to one another, laughing and joking. How could these people laugh and joke at a time like this? This was an aspect of dying that I did not like, and an aspect that I certainly did not want to learn about or remember. How dare they laugh, feel happy, or even smile at a time like this!

I walked away from everyone and stood near a little pond. I thought about Mrs. Usher and how she really loved to fish when she and her family would go to a nearby lake. She'd buy live bait on a Saturday and tell everyone that if the bait was still alive on Sunday morning, then God wanted her to fish. I guess it was God who told her to keep pouring fresh water into the bait bucket all night. Then she would ask God to forgive her for fishing on a Sunday. Now that's a real fisherwoman, and I'm sure God did not mind at all.

I looked over and saw Mr. Usher standing by himself, looking down at the casket. I saw how sad, lonely, and unhappy he looked. I had never hugged a man before, but I really wanted to hug him that day.

That was the day I learned just how much that man really cared about me; I never knew it before.

I slowly walked over and stood next to him but did not say a word. I couldn't get up enough nerve to tell him what I wanted to say. However, I knew I had to do something, and I had to do it quickly, because he was all I had left now that Mrs. Usher was gone.

I made my fists into a tight ball, then I said, "Dad, do you know how sad and lonely you feel right now?"

He nodded his head very slowly. I saw a tear, and he took my hand and squeezed it hard. Then he looked down at me.

I said, "Dad, that is how I have felt every single day of my life."

He grabbed me and hugged me tight.

"I know, boy."

When Mr. Usher died some years later, I still did not know how to act about it. So I stayed by myself in the little garden at the hospital until it was all over. I never did laugh or smile or joke like those other people.

I just couldn't.

Mr. Lucky

"**D**oes it hurt badly?" asked my wife, Dian, as we drove along.

"I'll be okay," I told her, even though the pain was excruciating.

Less than two weeks before, I'd undergone major surgery for cancer. The wound from the surgery extended from my breastbone almost to my legs. Although I'd received a pretty dire prognosis, I wasn't going to let this get the best of me. Nothing was going to keep me down.

After several hours of driving, we pulled into Reno, Nevada, and checked in at a motel for the night. Being in the gambling capital, I immediately thought of the $4,000 in cash that we had with us, and I imagined winning big and leaving a nice bundle of money behind for the family. I figured that trying my luck with just a couple hundred wouldn't hurt, and it would make a big difference, if I won.

"Would you mind if we went to a casino and gambled just a little bit?" I asked my wife. She smiled. "Just for a little while," she said.

We got everything settled and headed off to one of the casinos. I sat down at one of the tables and placed $100 on the table. The dealer immediately took the money and gave me chips. No matter what I did, however, I just could not win a hand at poker. Within thirty minutes, I'd lost my stake.

"Let's go back to the motel," said my wife.

"I really want to play. I really do," I told her.

Again, I lost another $100. I rose from my chair and smiled at my wife. She handed me two rolls of quarters, which I stuck into my pocket.

As we reached the motel, we started up the stairs to the second floor. I looked across the parking lot and saw an old man looking in a dumpster. I stood there for a moment, watching him.

"He's eating out of the dumpster," I said to my wife.

As quickly as I could, I walked back down the stairs and over to the man, who was leaning over the trash container. When I approached, I could see that he was eating the leftovers from a Kentucky Fried Chicken box.

"Please don't do that. Please don't," I said.

I reached in my pocket and took out the two rolls of quarters.

"Here. Please take this and get yourself something to eat."

"Thank you, Mr. Lucky," he said in a soft tone.

"Please don't buy anything to drink. Get yourself something to eat," I said.

He said not a word. I turned around and walked back to the motel, where my wife was standing. When I turned to look back at the old man, he was gone.

My wife and I went up to the room, and I tried to rest as best I could. After about thirty minutes, I looked over at my wife and said, "I really would like to play cards."

We put on our coats and went back to the casino. Once again I sat down at the card table. I took out another $100 and laid it on the table.

"Lowball," yelled the dealer, as he dealt out five cards to each player. I looked at my cards: I had an ace, a two, a three, a four, and a five. It is the lowest possible hand you can get when playing lowball.

All of a sudden the betting started. Within one round, my entire stack was in the pot. When the hand ended, I had won $800. When the cards were dealt again, I looked. Again I had an ace, a two, a three, a four, and a five.

"Fifty dollars to you," said a man, as he threw his chips into the pot.

I carefully separated my chips into fifty dollars piles.

"Your fifty and fifty more," I said.

The table became quiet. All eight men threw in the wager.

"And a hundred more to you," said the first man.

"And another two hundred to you," said another player.

I threw in the wager and sat there quietly.

"Let's see the cards, gentlemen," said the dealer.

Once again, I won—this time almost $2,000.

"Take the money, Clay," yelled a man, as he pushed his cards off the table and onto the floor.

I sat there for six hours and won eight out of ten hands. When the game was finally over, the casino stacked, trayed, and cashed in my chips for me. In the end, I won more than $16,000. That was more money than I had seen in my entire lifetime.

With my pockets full, my wife and I left the casino. Standing by the front door out in the cold was the same old man who had earlier been eating out of the dumpster.

"Can I buy you a mixed drink?" I asked.

The old man reached out and touched me gently

on the forehead. A very strange, warm, and calm feeling came over my entire body. All the pain from my surgery seemed to disappear in an instant.

"I don't drink, Mr. Lucky," said the old man, smiling at me.

I held out several one-hundred dollar bills, but he would not take anything.

"Mr. Lucky," he said again, shaking his head and then patting me on the back. Then he turned around and walked away into the night.

That was almost twenty-five years ago. Considering that the doctor had given me less than six months to live, I now know what the old gentleman meant when he called me Mr. Lucky.

The Medicine That Saved Me

"I'll be back in about half an hour," I said, as I walked out the front door.

Still quite sore from my cancer surgery, I began the one-mile walk to the drugstore to pick up my medicine.

Things had been a bit tough on my wife, Dian, and me ever since the welfare department had taken almost everything we owned. It was almost unbelievable that we owed nearly $100,000 in hospital bills. Our small trampoline business, our car, our wedding rings, and our money had all been confiscated by the county as partial payment of the large bill.

As I entered the pharmacy, I got in line to wait my turn. In front of me was an elderly woman who was giving the pharmacist a very hard time. Feeling a little sick to my stomach, I turned around and sat down on one of the six hard chairs in the small waiting area. Within a minute, the older woman also came over and sat down. I watched as she continually rubbed her legs. Almost in tears, she began to talk with me.

"This gout is killing me," she replied.

"I had a few bursts of that last year, in my feet," I told her.

"Then you know how it hurts."

"Yes, ma'am, I sure do."

The pharmacist interrupted. "Ma'am, there is nothing I can do for you. Your doctor is out of town, and there is no one I can possibly contact at this late hour. Besides, you're over your medication quota for the month, anyway."

"What type of medicine do you take?" I asked.

"Colcho—something or other," she tried to say.

"Colchicine," shouted a girl who was standing by the pharmacist.

"Ma'am, I have two or three full prescription bottles of that at home. I never used it but maybe two or three times. I mean—full bottles," I told her, in a quiet tone.

"How much do you want?" she replied.

"Nothing, you can have it."

"Thank you, dear. That is so kind of you," she replied.

"One problem, though," I told her.

She looked at me, her eyes opened wide.

"You will have to wait until I walk home and bring it back."

"Don't you have a car, sonny?"

"No, ma'am," I replied.

When my prescription was filled, I paid for it and walked to the front door. Sitting in a taxi cab was the elderly woman.

"Here's your ride home," she said, laughing, and then began coughing.

Within minutes we arrived at my small house.

The woman waited in the taxi while I hobbled into the house and dug out the pills from a cardboard box underneath the bathroom sink. I told my wife what I was doing and then walked out to the waiting cab and handed the woman the three bottles of medicine.

"Why would you do this for a total stranger?" the woman asked.

"I guess, because you need it. I don't need it anymore. It would just go bad sitting under the bathroom sink."

"Give me your phone number, young man."

We had no telephone, so I gave her the phone number of my in-laws, and the taxi driver wrote it down for her. As they drove away, she waved to me several times out the back window.

I went back into the house, took my own medications, and then stretched out on the bed to rest for a few minutes.

Within seconds, the medicine kicked in, and I was out for the remainder of the night.

Because we owned nothing of value, I had no idea how we were going to start a new life for ourselves. All night the dreams were haunting and terrible.

Early the next morning, someone knocked on our door. When my wife answered, there stood the elderly woman.

"Is that man here who gave me the medicine?"

"Hon, I think this is for you," shouted my wife. As I walked to the front door, Dian gave me a funny look.

"Young man, can you and the missus come with me?" she asked.

I stuck out my hands to let her know that I did not understand what she meant.

"Can you two come with me?" she stated again.

My wife walked back into the room to see what was going on.

"Hon, she wants us to go with her."

"Go where?"

"Just you two never mind," said the woman.

I looked outside and saw a taxi sitting in the driveway.

"Let's go," she said, as she put her hand into the small of my back.

We loaded into the taxi, and off we went.

We must have ridden for thirty minutes before the taxi finally drove up to a small farmhouse out in the country. The woman paid the taxi driver, and he drove away.

"How are we going to get home?" I asked the woman.

"You just let me worry about that," she replied.

We followed her out back to an old barn.

"Didn't you tell me yesterday that you don't own an automobile?"

"Yes, ma'am."

"Well, I am going to give you a car. Open those two barn doors," ordered the lady.

I looked at my wife, raised my eyebrows, and wondered what type of old junk car awaited us behind the two barn doors. When I opened the creaking doors, I looked inside, and right before me sat a brand-new Chevrolet station wagon. It was a little dusty, but not a scratch could be seen on it.

"I'm sorry, ma'am, but we cannot accept this," I told her.

"And just why not?" the woman asked.

"The county will just take it from us."

"Why would they do that?"

"I owe almost one-hundred-thousand dollars for the cancer surgery I had last month."

"How can they take your car?"

"We cannot own any vehicle that is less than three years old."

"Then there is no problem."

"What do you mean?" I asked her.

"This car is almost eight years old."

"It can't be. There are less than two-thousand miles on the odometer," I stated, as I opened the door and looked inside.

"My husband purchased this car in Fresno two days before he died. He made me promise that I would learn to drive and that I would never sell it."

"Then why aren't you driving it?"

"Never learned to drive," she said, chuckling aloud.

"But didn't he also tell you that you could never sell it?"

"I'm not selling anything. I'm giving it away. I'm sure that my late husband would approve."

After walking inside, the woman excused herself, telling us that she was going to retrieve the title from her safe. When she returned, she signed the station wagon over to us.

After hugging my wife and me, she bid us good-bye. She waved both her arms in the air as we drove down the dirt driveway.

This was the start of a new life for my wife and me. I remember thinking that this kind and gentle elderly woman, along with three useless bottles of pills, saved me. Once again, I set out on a new start.

The World It Is a-Changin'

My wife, Dian, and I left Modesto, California, and headed to Brunswick, Georgia, so I could start a new job I had taken several weeks earlier. Since our finances were tight, we sold what little we had accumulated over the past five years in order to make the 3,000-mile trip. With only about $200 in our pockets, we would have no fancy meals; maybe we'd have one night at a motel to take a shower and get a good night's sleep. The remainder of the time we would eat cheap burgers at McDonald's and sleep in our small car.

Even though I was tired, leaving a state behind always seemed to perk me up just a bit. When boredom set in, I would turn on the CB radio and listen to the truckers gab and yell at one another. When the language would get a little coarse, I would reach over and turn off the radio. About halfway through Texas, I reached over to turn off the radio when I heard "Is there anyone out there kind enough to help us?"

"Get off the truckers' channel, idiot," yelled a truck driver.

I reached over, picked up the microphone, and said, "What do you need?"

"We are stranded at mile marker 576, eastbound side," said a man.

I watched for the next mile marker sign, which read 574.

"I'm at 574 eastbound. What do you need?"

"Can you two idiots get off the truckers' channel?" said the trucker again.

I got no reply from the stranded man.

As I reached mile marker 576, there stood a black man beside an old brown van. I pulled up behind his vehicle, got out, and walked toward him. As I passed the van, I looked in and noticed about five elderly people.

"What's the problem?" I asked.

"Not sure. I can't find my wallet. I think I left it in the washroom at a restaurant about thirty miles back," he told me.

"What do you need?" I asked.

"You got any extra gas?"

"Just a minute," I said. I walked back to my car and explained the situation to my wife.

"We got just enough money to get us to Georgia, maybe. We can't afford to help anyone else," she replied.

"I can't just leave them stranded."

"Do what you got to do, hon," she said, shaking her head.

I walked back to the van, pulled out my wallet, and handed the man twenty dollars.

"You follow us back to the restaurant, and I'll give you the money back," said the man.

"I can't afford to go backward, I just can't," I told him.

He took my name and new address and promised to send me the money when he reached his home in Jackson, Mississippi.

I followed them to the next gas station and waved as they pulled up to the pump. Then we drove back onto the freeway and continued our journey.

"Are we going to make it, Roger?"

"I don't know," I said, biting my bottom lip.

Leaving Texas, we had had about sixty dollars left in our pockets. Now we knew for sure that there would be no bath and good night's rest at a motel.

As we continued through Louisiana, the traffic became heavy. Suddenly my wife screamed, and I looked up to see furniture falling off a pickup truck in front of us. I swerved to the right as quickly as possible, but I still ran over something. I got out of my car and walked to the front to see what damage had been done. Beneath the car was a small stereo system. It had cut through my right front tire, which was now flat. I walked to the trunk to get my jack and the spare tire and was shocked to see that it too was flat. Generally I check and recheck everything before going on a trip.

As I walked back to the front of my car, I saw that the driver of the pickup truck had reloaded what could be salvaged and that he was getting back into his vehicle. I knew that he had seen our flat tire, but he drove away, anyway.

My wife and I sat on the side of the road for several hours, waiting for the police. It was almost dark when they finally arrived. They advised us that there was nothing they could do other than call a tow truck. We knew that we could not afford to pay for such a service.

After the police left, we sat in the car wondering what to do.

I heard the honk of a horn. When I turned around to see what was happening, there was that same brown van and the people we'd given gas money.

"Well, I see we aren't the only ones having a little bad luck today," said the man, leaning into my window.

"No spare," I told him.

"Well, can't fix the problem sitting there," he said.

He reached over, took my keys out of the ignition, walked to the trunk of the car, and took out the jack. I watched him jack up the car and take off the flat. I didn't know what to say and was too embarrassed to tell him that we did not have enough money to buy a new tire and still have enough gas money to make it to Georgia.

After he took off the tire, he looked at me and said, "Go sit in the car, and I'll be right back."

I got into the car and watched them drive away.

"How we going to pay them, Roger?"

"I don't know. We'll just pay them for the tire and the repair to the flat."

"What we going to do for gas?"

"I don't know," I said, on the verge of screaming. "I just don't know."

The van returned an hour later. I got out of the car, noticing that the two tires the man had returned with were brand new.

"I'm sorry, but I should have told you. I don't have enough money to pay for two tires."

The man said nothing as he placed one tire on the car, acting as though he hadn't heard me.

"I'm sorry, but I—"

"I heard you the first time," he said.

Once the tire was on, he placed the jack and the new spare in the trunk and closed it.

"Follow us to the gas station," he ordered, sounding like an army sergeant.

We followed them to the next exit ramp and into the gas station. He got out of his van and began filling our tank. When he was done, he walked up to the window and said, "I'm hungry, let's eat." I looked at my wife, who was speechless for the first time in her life.

We followed them to a restaurant several blocks down the road. As we got out of the car, I looked at him and said, "Thank you for your help, but I cannot accept any more."

The man again said nothing. He walked back to his van, opened the side door, and took out a large wooden chair. Then he opened the passenger-side door, and out stepped the largest black woman I had ever seen in my life. I swear, the ground almost moved when she walked. The two of them walked over and stopped in front of me. The man, looking at me straight in the eyes, opened the folded chair and then stepped back. The big woman sat down, pointed at me, and said, "Johnny tells me I need to spank your little white butt. Is that going to be necessary?"

In total shock, my eyes opened wide, I replied, "No

ma'am," shaking my head vigorously.

"Good," she said, giving me a very stern look.

She smiled, then got up and walked toward the restaurant, along with the other people in the van. The man walked back to the van and replaced the chair.

It must have been almost 10:00 PM when we finally ate. Halfway through the meal, Johnny excused himself and was gone for more than twenty minutes. When he returned, he laid a motel key in front of me.

"I'm sorry, but I—"

"Mama," said Johnny in a harsh tone.

As the large woman started to stand up, I motioned for her to sit back down. I wouldn't argue.

As we ate, Johnny tapped his spoon against his glass. When everyone quieted down, he raised his glass of water and said, "I would like to make a toast. This is the way America should be." He almost choked on the words.

Everyone took a sip of water and sat there quietly, all smiling and nodding their heads.

After we had finished eating, we all walked to the motel next door. I shook Johnny's hand, and the large woman hugged me and my wife.

When Dian and I got up the next morning, their

van was gone. A white envelope was left on our windshield. Written on it was "Thank you and may God bless." Inside was a twenty-dollar bill, folded in the shape of a cross.

If Ever I Saw Your Face

My heart was pounding as I waited for the plane to land at Jacksonville International Airport. This would be the first time I had seen my daughter since she was two years old. She was now twenty-two.

This would be the first time in my life that I had ever seen anyone who had become an adult that I had known as a child. It's strange but true. Because I was raised in an orphanage till age fourteen, spent time in the juvenile court system and reform school, and then went to jail at the age of nineteen.

I had never stayed in one place long enough to ever see anyone grow up. This was a very unusual situation for me, and it was doubly difficult to deal with because it was my own daughter.

I watched every young woman's face as she disembarked. *Is that her? Or could that be her? No, that one must be her!* My eyes were open wider than they had ever been before, so that I would not miss her. My mind was racing at ninety miles per hour in a never-ending circle of confusion. *What is she going to think of me as a person, what will I look like to her as a father, and what will she look like?* Finally, there she came, walking straight toward me—the most beautiful sight I had ever seen. This thin blond work of art had the biggest smile I had ever seen.

"Dad?" she said, with a big smile on her face.

"Twila?" I responded, as I stared into her eyes.

We hugged each other for a brief moment and then started walking toward the luggage terminal to get her baggage. I could not help but stare at her constantly, and I hoped that she would not notice. It was just so amazing to me. Here was this unbelievable person walking beside me. This beautiful young woman was here on Earth because of me. I couldn't believe it. It was absolutely amazing.

I felt like jumping on top of one of the tall airport terminal chairs and yelling to the crowd, "Ladies and gentlemen, it moves, it walks, and it talks, just like a real live person!"

I was in a state of shock, but I tried to act as though it were no big deal. However, this was a big deal, and I was overwhelmed by fear and a strange sense of happiness. After leaving the airport, we stopped at a restaurant for supper. Then we got a motel room, where we sat for hours looking at the photo albums I'd brought with me. Finally, she fell asleep. I sat there on the chair beside the bed for hours and hours, just staring at her. I could not believe that she was real, that this was my daughter, that she was a part of me. It was like a miracle happening in front of my very eyes.

I took off my shoes and socks, placed my feet on the bed beside her, and tried to sleep. As I was about to doze off, I moved my foot toward her, and my heel touched her foot. It was so wonderful. Here was this warm, live, breathing human being. It was as though I had touched a part of me that I never knew existed. This unusual feeling radiated through my entire being, and it felt so strange and so unusual. I felt such pride that she was part of me.

That day was the beginning of my life as a father. It was the day that I started to learn how to be there for a precious child of mine. It was the day that I came to realize that I truly had a heart and a soul and that I was entitled to use it to love someone—especially my children.

Being a Good Father

Before I had grandchildren, I had never celebrated Father's Day. Why would I? I do not have the slightest idea who my father is. It's too far back to recall, and when I try to conjure up an image of my father, my mind goes totally blank. There are no memories of a father—or a mother, for that matter. All I remember is the orphanage and the reform school, and perhaps some of the kind people who cared for me occasionally.

I do not suppose that I was ever really bothered about the fact that I did not have parents. You must first know what something is in order to miss it. Since I never really had it, I never missed it. Having parents is not a matter of life and death. Neither is having children. I remember when my kids were born, but just bringing them into the world doesn't make someone a father. Thus, when I think back to when I truly became a father, it is not at the time of the birth of my children. My first two children, James and Kevin, were kept from me for almost fourteen years by their mother. I didn't see my third child, Twila, for nearly twenty years. My fourth child, Roger Jr., lived with me his entire childhood. He is married now, with two children of his own, and he lives next door to Judy, his stepmother, and me.

I have a hard time figuring out if I was a good father, because I did not have any role models. To me, raising children meant supplying a home, food, clothing, and an education and making sure that they brushed their teeth and did their homework. I also tried to share what little I knew about right and wrong. I tried to give my children whatever I could, and I knew enough never to raise my hand to them or degrade them, as had been done to me. I even took them swimming, fishing, boating, and camping. However, I did not read to them in bed. I did not hold them tenderly. I did not even tell them that I love them. So was I a good father?

My answer comes when I watch my son Roger interacting with my grandchildren. I watch him very closely and can plainly see the love on his face when he is with them. When he comes home from work and is greeted by his children, his face lights up the whole room. I know that he loves his children very much and that he would do anything for them. I smile when I hear him tell them that he loves them, and it is then that I know that I was—and I am—a good father.

Cinnamon

I left California many years ago, but hardly a day went by that I did not think about returning to fish for striped bass in the beautiful California Delta. Like many other people, I cannot afford an elaborate vacation. My social security disability check, together with my wife Judy's job as a waitress, will not allow us to head off to Rome or other fancy places. However, we had managed to save a little money, and my dream of again fishing in the California Delta waters was finally coming true.

The round-trip tickets would cost us less than $400, and two days of fishing would cost about $100 per day. In addition, Judy and I were invited to stay, at no charge, in the home of my friend Danny, who was in need of a liver transplant. With our round-trip airline tickets in hand and $400 in cash, off we flew to sunny California.

The first day of our vacation was spent with Danny and his wife, Lois, in Modesto. We talked, laughed, and made up for lost time in our friendship. Danny and Lois lived right on the edge of the airport district—squalid and dangerous, the kind of area where, if you're unknown, your personal safety is something you have to be very careful about. Nevertheless, on Tuesday morning I was up early and decided to take a stroll around the old neighborhood.

This was where my former in-laws had lived before their deaths. I noticed that not much had changed; poverty was still poverty. The teenage kids were still cursing and fighting with one another, and the gangs trotted down the street to see what they could steal from the local corner markets.

I slowly walked down the street until I got to the corner of Connie Way. I looked at the large water-filled holes and spotted the half-paved, pothole-ridden roadway filled with trash and mud—they looked just as they did thirteen years earlier. Halfway down the block, I saw the small shacklike house where my in-laws once lived. As I looked farther down the street, I could see ten or fifteen old broken-down junk cars lining the roadway, as well as tons of worthless old tires, large piles of trash, crushed tin cans, and broken glass bottles. It was desolate. Nothing would ever change here for 1,000 years or more. There was absolutely no color for the eye to see except a light gray. Everything looked totally barren of life.

I jumped as I felt something rub against my leg. When I looked down, I saw a small cinnamon-colored cat. I could hardly believe my eyes when I saw that the cat's leg was severely injured. I picked the animal up in my arms, carried it back to Danny's house, and gave it food and water. I watched as the cat ate the food, gulping every bite as though she hadn't eaten or had anything to drink in days.

The small cat had a broken leg, which was swollen, and she was dragging her entire foot behind her as she walked. I immediately called a veterinarian and explained the situation. I was told that he would not take a stray cat unless there was someone who would take full responsibility for payment of the treatment.

After we visited another veterinarian and agreed to pay a twenty-five-dollar fee, the cat was examined. We were told that the cat's foot was broken and that its leg had almost been twisted completely off. Amputation of the entire leg from the shoulder down was the only recourse. We were also told that the injury must have happened at least a week or two ago, because the infection had spread into the shoulder. The vet told us that the charge for removing the entire leg would be about $1,000.

Unable to pay the high fee, Judy and I took the cat back to our room. We tried to make it as comfortable as possible throughout the night. The next morning, I walked down to the corner store, where I learned that earlier in the week, four young boys had twisted a cat's leg until it broke and then smashed its foot with an old car starter. They shot it in the back of the neck with a pellet gun and buried it half alive.

Judy and I stayed on the phone for hours trying to find a vet to help us save the animal, but to no avail. Danny finally came into our room and told us it was a hopeless case and that we should just have the cat put to sleep. However, I couldn't do that.

"Dan, if I ever accomplish anything in my life, I will save at least one thing from the airport district," I told him.

Danny looked at me with tears in his eyes and said, "Roger, that is why we have been friends for so many years. You just never give up when it comes to fixing something that is broken or hurt."

By the end of the day, a surgeon at the Modesto Spay and Neuter Clinic agreed to amputate Cinnamon's leg at cost, which totaled $377.84.

Judy and I gave up our fishing trip and used the money toward Cinnamon's medical expenses. Sonny's Real Pit BBQ threw in fifty dollars. Our friend Sharen, though she had many bills because of breast cancer surgery, contributed $130, and my son Roger pitched in $100.

The wonderful people at Delta Airlines refused to accept the normal seventy-five-dollar fee for pets to travel. They insisted that Cinnamon fly home with Judy and me for free. Cinnamon now lives here with us at our home in Georgia.

Here was an innocent little animal who never hurt anyone. She had her leg broken, almost torn away, and now amputated. She had been shot in the head with a pellet gun and then buried alive by four people who call themselves human beings. In spite of all of her suffering, Cinnamon still had the heart to hobble up to a strange man standing on a street corner in a place like a war zone and rub up against him to let him know that she still loves human beings. This is the most amazing lesson of all: don't judge all people by the actions of some.

It is not Cinnamon or the people mentioned in this story who are the heroes here. The true hero in this story is the spirit of goodness and the spirit of kindness shown by the people. It's a wonderful, wonderful feeling that lives deep in the hearts of most good, kind, and decent people; it's a special feeling that makes an honest-to-goodness hero appear when a real hero is needed.

The Party

After finishing three hours of taping for a television special on U.S. orphanages, I loosened my tie and headed for my car. Before leaving Florida, I decided to drive by a few of the areas in which I had hung around as a young boy. Jacksonville sure has changed, I said to myself, as I drove from one area to another.

There was a time when I used to walk from one side of Jacksonville to the other—one mile, ten miles, maybe even twenty miles. Distance seemed to make no difference to me when I was a boy. Many times I had just run away from the orphanage; I would eat what I could find in the dumpsters, and I would sleep in abandoned red brick buildings along the avenue.

I drove over to Post Street and walked up to the apartment where I'd been molested by a schoolteacher who allowed me to spend the night with him. Next I drove to Spring Park School, which was located next door to the orphanage. I parked and walked over to the orphanage property. I stood there, looking through the six-foot-high chain-link fence. Other than a few new buildings, nothing had changed. All was quiet and still. There was absolutely no sign of life, and there was no laughter to be heard anywhere.

Next, I drove downtown to see the old rooming house where I had lived as a teenager. To my surprise, it was gone, and a skyscraper stood in its place. I parked, then walked and walked until my legs began to hurt. I rested for several minutes against a department store window, watching the cars as they passed.

How well I remember those red taillights, I thought. *Thousands upon thousands of red lights all headed to who knows where.*

It was now past dark, so I thought that I should head back home to Georgia.

Maybe I'll stop in and have one drink before I hit the freeway, I said to myself.

I walked a block or two, looking for an open lounge. As I rounded the corner, there stood a man in a suit and tie holding a door open.

"Are you here for the party? Free food and drink," he blurted out.

I looked in the doorway and saw about fifty people.

All were laughing, holding drinks, and dressed to kill.

"Can you smoke?" I asked the man.

"No smoking allowed in Jacksonville inside any building."

"I'll finish this cigarette, and I might be in," I stated.

"What's life without a party?" said the man, as he closed the door and walked away to join the others.

I stood there, puffing away at my cigarette. Suddenly, I saw flames coming from an alley between two large buildings. I walked across Market Street and looked down the alley. I could see four or five people standing around a fifty-five-gallon drum that had a fire burning in it.

I stopped, turned around, and looked back at the doorway where the man had invited me to the party.

Free drinks, free food, and intelligent company, I thought.

I stood there for a moment, then I looked back at the fire. I began to walk slowly toward the alley.

"Mind if I join you?"

"You a cop?" someone asked.

"No. I'm just plain old me."

No one said a word as I walked up and began warming my hands over the fire. I noticed a few eyes looking at me every now and then.

"You from around here?" asked a large heavyset woman.

"No, ma'am."

"Ma'am! Ain't anybody called me 'ma'am' for a long time."

The four men began to laugh.

"Sorry," I told her.

"Don't be sorry," she said rather quickly.

I stood there warming my hands. I remember standing around many a fire as a runaway boy.

I did not know these people, but I had known many like them. Many times such people had fed me when I was hungry. They had given me warmth when I was cold. They had given me friendship when I was lonely.

"You got a cigarette I can borrow?" asked the woman.

"No, but I have a cigarette that you can have."

Again the men laughed.

When I held out the package, each person began taking a cigarette, and within five seconds I had fewer than five left from an almost full pack.

I pulled out my cigarette lighter and began to light everyone's cigarettes. Then I closed it and put it back into my pocket. I placed my own cigarette into my mouth, bent over, and lit it from the roaring fire.

"You've done this before. I can tell," said the woman.

"Done this many times, many years ago."

For the next two hours, we talked, laughed, and joked. I was a little uncomfortable with a few of the coarse jokes because there was a woman present, but she seemed to enjoy them.

Occasionally, I would notice a Cadillac drive up and drop guests off at the party across the street. I would watch the women in their full-length gowns enter the building. Then I would look over at the heavy woman in a wool overcoat and unmatched tennis shoes.

"You want to pitch in and get something to drink?" asked one of the men.

I had about $200 in my wallet and wasn't sure if I should pull it out.

"How much are we talking about?" I asked.

"Fifty cents each should do it."

I reached into my pocket and handed the fifty cents to the man. I watched as each gave him a share.

"You want to come?" he asked.

"Sure, why not?"

When we arrived at the liquor store, the man walked right over and picked up a bottle of the cheapest wine. I followed him to the counter, and we waited in line. As I stood there, I noticed a package of clear plastic champagne glasses with push-on pedestals. I reached over and picked up the package. When the cashier got to me, he looked at the wine and the glasses.

"I see you fellows are going to have a real fancy party," he said, as he rolled his eyes back and laughed.

"As a matter of fact, we are," I stated.

I pushed the bottle of wine to the side and instructed the clerk to give us the largest bottle of Crown Royal that he had in the store.

When we returned to the alley, I was surprised that no one said a word about the Crown Royal. I opened the box and removed the bottle from the purple pouch.

"Can I have that there cigarette bag?" asked one of the men.

I threw him the pouch, and he stood there rubbing it against his face. For the next four hours, the six of us stood around the fire, talking and telling stories. I watched as each person carefully and slowly sipped his or her drink. They all drank as if they were high society and had not a care in the world.

Then a police car pulled up at the entrance of the alley and threw a spotlight in our direction.

"Let's break it up and get out of there," said a policewoman, over the cruiser's radio system.

Without saying a word, everyone started walking down the alley in the opposite direction from the police car. I threw my plastic glass into the fire and began walking toward the police officers. As I passed them, neither said a word to me. I just nodded my head and walked across the street. I stepped onto the sidewalk, lit a cigarette, and just stood there, looking down the alley. Behind me, a door opened and the man who had invited me to the party came walking out with several other guests.

"How did you enjoy the party?" he asked.

"As a matter of fact, it was one of the best parties I've attended in years."

"Good," he said. "What good is life without a good party and good friends, right?" he continued.

"You are so right, my friend," I said, and I smiled.

Remembering the Feeling

It was very early, and hardly anyone was on the street. I parked my truck and searched for a phone booth to get the number for the barber college I was looking for in my old neighborhood. I had fond memories of going there as a child for a free haircut, so I thought I'd pay it a visit while I was in town.

It was rather cold, so I put on my coat and began searching for a telephone. A block down, I found an open shoe store. I went inside and asked if I could use the telephone book. Not finding a listing for the barber college, I picked out the number of a local beauty salon, hoping that someone there might be able to tell me if the barber college was still in business. The number was busy, so I decided to wait and try again in a few minutes.

"How about moving on down the road?" said the salesman in a loud harsh tone.

I turned to see if he was talking to me.

"Damn homeless guy always wanting to use our bathroom," he replied.

I saw a poorly dressed man standing outside the store, gazing through the large plate-glass window. The salesman motioned at the man with his hand in a backward motion, telling him to move on down the street.

Several more times I tried to dial the number, but it was continually busy.

"Like a cup of coffee?" the salesman asked me.

"That sounds great. Thanks."

As he and I stood there talking, the front door opened, and a man who looked about twenty years old came into the store. He was pushing himself in a wheelchair.

The salesman set down his coffee cup and walked toward the young man.

"I need a new pair of shoes," said the customer.

As he turned the corner, I noticed there was a blanket across his lap. I was shocked to see that the young man had no legs.

The salesman stood there, having no idea what he should say.

"A gift for a friend?" I asked the boy.

"No," he replied. "They are for me," he continued, with a smile on his face.

I just smiled back and watched to see what would happen next.

"What type of shoe would you like?" asked the clerk.

"How 'bout a pair of cowboy boots? You got any cowboy boots in here?"

The man pointed to the back wall where three or four pairs of boots were displayed.

"Let me have a look-see at those black ones in a size ten."

The salesman turned around sharply and headed off to the back room.

"Isn't this fun?" the boy asked me.

"You mean going into a shoe store when you have no legs and seeing the response?" I replied.

"Of course not."

I moved my hand to let him know that I did not understand his question.

"When I was a kid, my parents used to buy me a new pair of shoes every year. That was such a wonderful feeling, something I have never forgotten—the smell of the leather and the pride I felt when I walked around the store, showing off my new shoes."

The salesman came back down the aisle with a large box. He set it down on the floor, took out a single boot, and handed it to the young man. The boy closed his eyes, placed the boot against his nose, tilted his head backward, and drew in a large breath.

I did not know what to say as tears began to stream down the young man's cheeks.

"What type of accident did you have?" I asked him.

"Farming," he said, as he tried to clear his voice.

"Move on down the road," yelled the salesman, as he once again motioned his hand at the homeless fellow looking in the window.

The youngster looked at the old man and then turned to face me.

"Will you walk out there and see what size shoes that fellow wears?" he requested.

I slowly walked to the front door, opened it, and asked the old man to come in.

"What size shoes do you wear?" the boy asked the man.

"I don't know," he replied, as he looked down at his old tennis shoes.

"I would say about a nine and a half," I replied.

"What's your best hiking boot in nine and a half?" the boy asked the clerk.

The salesman turned and once again walked to the back of the store.

The homeless fellow stood there, looking down at the floor.

Within a minute, the clerk returned with a pair of hiking boots, the insides lined with wool. The boy reached out, took a boot, placed it to his nose, and drew in a large breath. Once again, tears came to his eyes.

"Sir, would you mind trying on these boots for me?" the boy asked the old fellow, as he held out the boot.

The old man sat down, used his feet to slide off his tennis shoes, and took the boot. The boy motioned for the clerk to aid him. The salesman slid his small knee-high seat in front of the man and began tying the bootstraps.

The old man's eyes never left the floor the entire time. After the boots were tied, the young boy asked the gentleman if he would walk around so that he could see the boots at a distance.

"How do they feel?" he asked the man.

"They feel wonderful," replied the man.

"I'll take 'em," the young boy told the clerk.

"Those are one-hundred-and-eighty-nine-dollar boots," the clerk advised the boy.

The boy pulled out his wallet and handed the clerk two $100 bills.

"Do you want the cowboy boots?" the salesman asked him.

"I don't think so."

"Don't you have to use the bathroom?" I asked the old man.

He stood up and walked toward the back of the store. The clerk motioned his head, giving him the okay.

"I see that buying a new pair of shoes still gives you that good feeling you talked about," I told the young man, as I smiled.

"Yes, it does." he said. "And now I have some feet to share it with."

We had just lost to old age two more of the many animals we'd saved over the years from abusive situations. I was not in the mood to take on any more, mainly because of the high veterinary costs. Besides, we'd been rescuing animals for ten years, and it had caused us many hardships.

As my wife, Judy, and I were driving near the airport, she suddenly turned into the Glynn County Animal Shelter and came to a stop.

"What are we doing here?" I asked her.

"I'm not sure," she replied.

I watched as she opened her door and began walking toward the fenced building. I had a sinking feeling.

"Going to come in with me?"

"I'm not going in there," I said as firmly as I could.

I watched as she disappeared into the large white building.

There was something about dog pounds that I

hated. Maybe it was seeing dogs locked in cages. Maybe it was the sounds of the animals wanting to be rescued and loved. These are feelings that I had known very well as an abused little boy.

"Roger," yelled Judy, several minutes later.

When I turned around, I saw her standing in a small fenced area, and a midsize black and tan dog was jumping all over her. I got out of the truck and walked over to the fence.

"Isn't he beautiful?" she asked.

I just shook my head and began walking back to the truck.

"Will you please come in here?" she hollered.

I stopped, turned around, and began walking toward the main building. Once inside, I was led down a long hallway. Dogs were barking everywhere; it was almost deafening. As I walked along, I tried not to look at the hundreds of animals howling and barking at me—some sullen, some wagging their tails and smiling. I tried to push away thoughts like "Cheer up, or you're not getting out of here, buster."

As an attendant led me into the small fenced viewing area where Judy was waiting, the dog began to jump on me. When I ran my hand down his back, I noticed a large scar. I asked the attendant what had caused the injury. She told me that he had been beaten with a metal coat hanger. I felt my neck begin to swell, and my throat began to tighten. Many times in the orphanage I, too, had been beaten with such an instrument. I began walking very quickly toward the main entrance, to get out of the building as soon as possible.

"His name is Sam, and he is going to be put down tomorrow!" yelled Judy.

"We just can't afford to save any more animals," I whispered.

Unable to speak, I walked to the truck, closed and locked the door, and wiped my burning red eyes.

In my heart there was a brutal battle talking place—one that I knew I would lose. Nevertheless, it was one I had to fight.

As Sam lies on the bed between my wife and me tonight, for some reason he begins to lick the scars on my leg. In the faint light of the television, I reach over and pat him on his large scar, and I whisper, "Yes, I am Sam."

A Rose Is a Weed Is a Rose

Seeing a United Parcel Service truck pulling into my driveway, I opened the garage door. I knew that another package had arrived helping us with the Christmas in July party we were putting together for the children at a local orphanage.

As I stood watching the driver get the packages from the back of the truck, I saw Madison, my three-year-old granddaughter, picking weeds from the lawn.

"These are for my mommy and daddy," she stated, as she held out a handful of worthless little weeds. I smiled and nodded as I looked at her tight little closed fist.

The UPS driver walked into the garage and set the two packages on a wooden bench. He and I talked about the numerous baseball gloves, baseball bats, helmets, and baseballs strewn about the room. I told him that I'd been raised in a Jacksonville orphanage and that during my entire childhood I had never owned anything. I told him that these presents were for the children themselves and not for the orphanage.

After talking for a few minutes, the driver told me that he had to leave. He waved and walked back down the driveway. I turned around, locked the garage door, and walked up onto the front porch. Just as I closed the dog gate, Madison came running up to where I was standing.

"My flowers, my flowers," she shrieked.

I soon realized that I had locked her weeds in the garage. "We'll get them later," I told her. I didn't want to walk back down the stairs and unlock the garage door for a bunch of worthless weeds. It just was not worth the effort.

Putting my hand onto her small shoulder, I began directing her back into the house. After walking about ten feet, I stopped dead in my tracks.

You can walk out to the garage for the kids in the orphanage, but you can't walk to the garage for your granddaughter? I kept thinking. *Those weeds are beautiful flowers to your granddaughter just as those baseball gloves are like gold to those orphan children.*

I turned around, walked back to the end of the porch, and opened the dog gate. Then I walked down the three stairs, took out my keys, and opened the garage door. Madison ran past me, grabbed the little treasures, which she had picked but moments before, and stood there smiling. I knelt down and looked through the green, now drooping and lifeless weeds, and I smiled as I saw the beauty of a dozen beautiful red roses reflected in her eyes.

The Prince and the Princess

"Is that your princess dress?" I asked my three-year-old granddaughter, Madison, as she walked out of her bedroom, dragging the trail of the dress behind her.

"Yes," she answered softly, with a sweet smile.

"And just where is your magic wand?"

She opened her hands to show that they were empty and said, "You got to make one for me."

A warm feeling always comes over me when she does something sweet or cute, and it always coaxes a smile out of me. Too often, however, that warm feeling is followed by an overwhelming sadness. I look at her innocence, and I wonder why no one at the orphanage had any of those feelings for us innocent children. Then I think about all the other small children today who are unloved by their caretakers.

I cannot recall ever pretending to be a prince or even wanting to be one. By the time I learned of such things, my young spirit had already been broken by the unloving manner in which I was "cared" for.

After a few more words passed between us, I kissed little Madison good-bye, and I closed my son's front door and walked next door to my house. I quickly changed my clothes and headed to the local hardware store. I gathered the items I thought I would need and rushed back to my garage. Feeling rather sly, I worked in secrecy for several hours as I crafted two magic wands—each eighteen inches long, topped by a large glittering star. One was made of gold for the princess, and one was made of silver for the prince.

The next morning, when Madison arrived at our house for us to babysit, this sixty-year-old prince, with an old torn towel draped over his shoulders, and his three-year-old princess played in the cardboard castle on the screened-in front porch.

It's never to late to be a prince, if someone would just open his eyes and realize that there's a princess in his own family who needs one.

The Monster

I cannot count the hours I spent locked in the orphanage closet when I was a child. The closet was dark, cold, and frightening. There were many terrible monsters lurking in every corner. For some strange reason, they never ate me. They just made crackling sounds, causing me to jump and shiver with fear almost all night long.

I've learned that monsters lived only in my mind as a child. However, because they were invisible, they were still very frightening. Even though I am now sixty-two years old, I recognize they can still be very alive in the imagination of a child.

My telephone rang at about 8:30 PM on Christmas Eve. It was my son, asking what he should do with my four-year-old granddaughter, Madison. He explained that when she was in bed, she heard a monster in her closet and began screaming. He told me that he opened the closet door to show her that there was nothing there. Nevertheless, she did not believe him.

I dressed as quickly as I could, drove to their apartment, and walked into Madi's bedroom.

"Papa heard you got a big monster problem over here." I told her.

"He's big, and he's scary, Papa. Real scary, and I real scared, too."

"Well, what do you think we should do?" I asked her.

"I don't know what to do, Papa. He's like invisible, sorta like."

"Well, if he's invisible, then we can't shoot him."

"Yeah, 'cause it'll go right through him."

"Honey, tell your daddy to give us a pencil and a great big piece of paper."

I watched as she jumped off the bed and scurried out the door to find her father. Several minutes later she walked back into the room, holding almost a full ream of copy paper.

Sprawled on her bed, we began to list the ways to get rid of the monster, then figure out which would be best. After five or ten minutes, we had decided that bullets, knives, rope, Drano, and Dora the Explorer could not solve our problem. Even the police, the fire department, ghost busters, Papa, and her daddy had been marked off the list.

"Papa, we gotta figure this out, and real quick sorta like," she advised me.

I took her by the hand, and we went into the kitchen. We looked through every drawer, trying to find something that would get rid of the monster. In the bathroom, we looked through every drawer and cabinet. There was nothing to be found that would solve our problem.

"Madi, you go look in that closet right there and see if there is anything that might help us," I told her.

Winking at her dad, I watched as she slowly and very carefully opened the small closet door.

"Papa, come over here."

Walking to her location, I watched and listened in amazement as she pointed to the vacuum cleaner and began to explain how the invisible monster could be sucked into the vacuum cleaner bag. She and I rolled the vacuum into her bedroom and I plugged it into the outlet. I motioned for her to remain perfectly quiet by placing my finger to my lips. I took a large plastic garbage bag, tore it in half, and taped the bag to each side of the closet door with masking tape, leaving only a small crack at the bottom for the vacuum hose to be slid into the closet.

"Hit the switch, kid, and let's suck the guts out of this here booger," I yelled.

As the vacuum came on, I quickly jammed the hose into the small plastic crack.

The two of us sat for almost five minutes without saying a word.

"I don't think he's going in the bag, Papa."

I carefully pushed the hose a little farther into the closet. Suddenly we heard something bang against the hose and fall into the bag.

"We got him," she yelled.

I ran over, jerked the plug out of the wall, and ran out the bedroom door. We ran as fast as we could through the kitchen and into the living room.

"Hurry, get the front door," I yelled at my son.

The three of us headed out the door and ran into the front yard.

Madison's eyes were as big as saucers as I began to remove the large vacuum bag.

"Are you going to let him go, Papa?" she asked in a scared tone.

"No way! We are going to make sure he never, ever comes back."

I removed the bag, wadded it into a tight ball, and took out my cigarette lighter. Holding the bag away from myself, I set it on fire and held it as long as I could before dropping it to the ground. The three of us stood there silently, watching as the monster disappear forever.

As I walked Madi back to her bedroom, I asked her if she wanted to check the closet before she went back to bed. She smiled and shook her head.

"Papa, thank you for getting rid of the monster," she said in a low tone.

"You're the one who figured out how to get rid of it," I said, smiling.

"Does that make me smart?"

"It sure does, and no monster will ever mess with you again. Monsters are afraid of you now, kiddo."

She smiled, tucked herself into a tight ball, and closed her eyes.

I kissed her on the cheek and headed back out to the front yard to retrieve what was left of the monster: a marble, a small heart-shaped candy, and a large paper clip.

A Very Expensive Mouse

With coffee in hand, I walked into my small home office so I could begin answering some of the many e-mails I generally receive each morning. I was surprised to see that the mouse on my computer was not functioning correctly. No matter what I tried, nothing seemed to correct the problem. Putting on my hat, I walked to my truck and drove to the local office supply store to purchase another mouse. After arriving, I began to look at the various types and was rather surprised at the price differences; some cost as much as sixty-four dollars!

Only an idiot would pay that much for a damn mouse, I thought.

After purchasing a nice-looking mouse for less than fifteen dollars, I headed back home. Little did I know that this was going to be a very small price to pay.

Less than an hour later, I was sitting in my office when I heard my wife, Judy, scream. Jumping up, I ran into the kitchen to see what had happened. There she stood, motionless, one hand over her mouth and the other pointing at the bottom of the refrigerator. A small mouse was sitting there, eating a small crust of bread.

"Get it out of here!" Judy screamed, just as someone knocked on the front door.

"You see who that is," I told her, "and I'll take care of this."

I slowly and carefully moved toward the broom in the corner. Grabbing the handle, I raised it above my head, and with all my might I slammed the broom toward the floor. I missed the mouse, however, and it scurried into another corner of the kitchen.

"I wanna see the little mousey," shrieked Madison, our four-year-old granddaughter, as she ran toward me.

"You stay back. These things can be very dangerous if they bite you," I warned her.

Again I raised the broom and took another swipe, and again I missed.

"Please don't kill it, Papa," yelled little Madi.

"You stay back, little lady," I warned her again.

"Please, please, please don't kill it," she begged.

I slowly lowered the broom and looked at her quivering little face.

"What am I supposed to do?" I asked my wife.

"Can we catch it and take it out where we go camping?" Madison asked.

"That's over an hour away, almost sixty miles," I blurted out.

"Please, Papa. Don't kill it," she continued to beg.

Setting the broom down in the corner, I walked into the bedroom and picked up a clear plastic file container. Stacking the folders on the bed, I returned to the kitchen and put the container on the floor. I winked at Madison, then made a jab at the mouse with the broom. Sure enough, it ran into the plastic box. I quickly turned the container upright and slammed on the lid.

Within minutes, the mouse, Madison, and I were in the truck and driving down the freeway, toward the Blythe Island Campground.

"Thank you, Papa, for not killing that little mousie."

I just smiled and winked.

Noticing that I was almost out of gas, I pulled off the freeway and into a convenience store, where I purchased eleven gallons of gas, two small bottles of orange juice, and a small bag of potato chips, all for twenty-nine dollars and fifty-seven cents. Then we got back on the freeway. Twenty six miles, later we pulled into the campground and stopped by the large lake. Picking up the container, Madison and I walked to the lake's edge. Making her stand back, I removed the lid and watched as the mouse hurried quickly into the tall bushes.

The smile on my granddaughter's face was worth $1 million.

Much to our surprise, the mouse came back out of the tall bushes and stood up on its hind legs.

"What's mouses eat, Papa?" asked Madison.

"Cheese, I think."

"Can we give him some cheese?"

"We don't have any cheese."

"Then what's he gonna eat?"

"I don't know."

"Papa, he'll die without no right kind of food."

"There's no place to get cheese around here," I told her.

"There's cheese at that store where we stopped back down the road."

"I'm not driving all the way back to that store."

Once again her mouth began to quiver and her eyes began to water.

"Get in the truck."

Suddenly she burst into tears.

"In the truck," I said, very sternly, as I pointed toward the vehicle.

Not a word was spoken between us as we traveled down the freeway. Out of the corner of my eye I could see the tears slowly running down her cheeks. As I approached the exit where we had previously gassed up, I decided to pull off and purchase a little more gas before returning home.

"Would you like another orange juice?" I asked her.

She nodded silently.

"You go get two more juices," I told her.

I began talking with the cashier as I waited for Madison. Feeling her tug at my shirt, I looked down. In her arms were two small bottles of orange juice and six packs of cheese and crackers.

With a sigh of disgust, I took the merchandise and placed it on the counter.

"That will be thirty-three dollars and thirty-four cents," said the clerk. Pulling out my credit card, I paid the charge. I was now sixty-three into this little venture.

We returned to the campground but we could not find the mouse, so we scattered the crackers on the ground around the bushes.

"Thank you for being good and kind, Papa," said Madi, as we walked back to the truck.

"Sometimes it is you who makes me want to be good and kind," I told her.

"Maybe when we come camping next year, we'll see him again. Maybe that mouse will grown up to be a great big rat. Big like a dog, maybe."

"Yeah. That'll work, all right."

As we returned home, we drove by the office supply store I'd been in earlier, and I remembered thinking, *Only an idiot would pay sixty-four dollars for a damn mouse.*

The Anniversary Present

Every year on our anniversary, my wife, Judy, and I celebrate the special occasion by having bacon, lettuce, and tomato sandwiches for dinner. This is a tradition we have held for fourteen years, because that is what we ate together the day we met.

About three o'clock on the day of our anniversary, Judy and I headed to Harvey's Grocery Store to purchase the ingredients for our celebratory meal. When I pulled into the parking lot, an elderly man and woman were driving about one mile per hour in the car in front of us. I became a little agitated.

"If I ever get that slow, I want you to shoot me in the damn head," I told my wife.

"Look, grandfather, you're already that slow," Judy replied, with just a hint of a smile.

I raised my eyebrows. "Well, then, forget it."

The old fellow pulled into a handicapped space, and the two slowly exited their automobile. By the time we parked, the elderly couple was heading into the store, the woman with a walker and the man with a three-legged walking cane. Judy and I were in the store well before them.

After we picked out a crispy head of iceberg lettuce and several juicy tomatoes, we headed to the meat counter for a slab of bacon. As we rounded the corner, we found ourselves right behind the elderly couple, pushing their shopping cart at maybe three feet per hour. Judy and I waited for them to move down the aisle so we could get to the bacon.

With shaking hands, the old man reached down and picked up a small package of pork chops. Holding them out to his wife, he said, "How about pork chops for our anniversary, Mother?"

She narrowed her eyes ever so slightly and replied, "You know we can't afford that, Dad."

The man placed the package back on the meat counter, and the two of them continued down the aisle. Judy picked out a large package of bacon, and we headed toward the bread aisle. As we passed the elderly couple, the man was reaching for a large package of hamburger meat.

"The small package, Dad. The small package," his wife told him.

Judy and I stopped and looked at each other.

"James Ditty time?" she asked, smiling.

"I think so, *Mom*," I said, smiling back at her.

We headed back to the meat counter and rang the buzzer. Several moments later, our friend James Ditty came out of the freezer.

"Hey, guys," he said, always glad to see us, and we him.

"James, how about four of your best center-cut pork chops, maybe one and a half inches thick?" Judy requested.

"You got it."

Judy and I waited as James cut and wrapped the meat. When he returned, I took the marking pen from his pocket and wrote "Happy anniversary" on the white package.

"How are we going to do this without embarrassing them?" Judy asked.

"Don't worry, I got it covered."

We turned down the bread aisle, picked out a loaf of bread, and headed to the checkout counter. After paying for our groceries, I took the pork chops and wrapped them in a plastic bag. I pointed out the elderly couple to the cashier and told her to slip the meat in their grocery bag when they checked out.

We stood up front and waited for the couple to come through the register. As the elderly woman fumbled through her purse, the cashier placed the pork chops at the bottom of their grocery bag and set the sack in their cart.

As they headed toward the front door, the old man was trying to push the shopping cart with one hand and hold his cane with the other.

"Can I help you with that?" I asked.

"Why, thank you, sonny."

As the "hours" passed, we finally made it the fifty feet to their automobile.

"Did I hear you say it's your anniversary today?" I asked the gentleman.

"Fifty-three years today."

"Fourteen for us," I told him.

"Well, happy anniversary," he said, with a grin.

"And a happy anniversary to you guys, too."

Judy and I watched as the two of them slowly made their way out onto Perry Lane Road. As car after car began to line up behind them, horn after horn began to blow.

"Thank you for the anniversary present, *Dad*. It's the best one you ever bought me."

I just looked at my wife, winked, and smiled.

Conclusion

I am amazed that the kindness of others has lasted me a lifetime. I did not understand how *love* was supposed to feel, but *kindness* I understood. Affection and love were not part of my upbringing, so I never became a truly affectionate man. However, I have always tried to be kind to others, since that, I guess, was the way I learned to express my feelings best. Love has very little effect on me, but kindness brings a tear to my eye every time.

Many people wonder how I managed to succeed after having survived the abusive orphanage and reform school and then prison. How did I manage to make a life for myself without the guidance of a loving family or friends? It was not an easy road to travel. The kindness that I experienced along the way helped me some, but I will be the first to admit that I am nowhere near perfect. When we are feeling sick in mind or body, we tend not to treat others as well as we would if we had just learned that we won the lottery. However, the world we face is pretty much the same every day that we get out of bed in the morning. The only real difference is how we feel, physically and mentally. Whether the day is going to be a sick day or a lottery day is strictly decided by us. I choose lottery days as often as possible.

I suspect that it is so important for me to be kind to others because the pain I suffered as a child was so deep and hurtful that I do not want others, especially children, to have such feelings. I could say that the man I am today is a result of the kindness that was shown to me, but that is not entirely true. The hurt and the heartache I endured is actually a large part of why I am successful today. Being called all sorts of foul words—*dumb*, *stupid*, *ignorant*, *bastard*, and so on—made me think that there was truth to those things and that I had to succeed to prove those words false. There was no way that I could take the chance that they might be right. So I succeeded.

Over the course of my life, I have been an orderly, a medic, an emergency medical technician, a licensed practical nurse, an army private, an army captain, a plumber, a carpenter, a printer, an army ammunitions inspector, a district manager, an artist, a painter, a child advocate, a cable installer, a telephone repairman, a cowboy, a cab driver, a tractor operator, a skating rink manager, a motel manager, an apartment manager, a parole officer, a legal representative, a jail-house lawyer, and a webmaster. I have also owned and operated several businesses.

Considering that I never finished the seventh grade, this is almost unbelievable. However, I take pride in the fact that I have excelled at every job I have had. I didn't work so many jobs because I was trying to find work. Rather, I was trying to find out who I was as a person. Who and what was I supposed to be in the world?

One night, more than a dozen years ago, before I went to bed, I mumbled, "Tomorrow morning when I get up, for the first time in my life, I am going to be me."

The next morning I looked directly at my reflection in the bathroom mirror and stared eye to eye at myself. Finally, I got up the nerve to ask, "Just who the hell are you? Are you the plumber, the lawyer, the garbage man, the nurse . . . ?"

As I stood there, I came to the realization that those things were *what* I was and not *who* I was. That was the day that the beady-brained, ugly little boy from the orphanage sat down at his computer and starting writing his first book. I realized then that to truly express myself through my words, I had to figure out *who* I was. I could feel nothing. I leaned back in my chair and thought about the orphanage, the reform school, and the system that had done me wrong. Anger and hatred rose to the surface. This confused me, because I had become a man with a very kind heart.

Eventually, through writing my stories, I realized that I had many stories stored in my head about good things that had happened to me, things that had touched my heart. I smile when I recall a dirty old hobo who shared his can of Spam with little Roger Dean Kiser when he was cold, tired, and scared. A tear comes to my eye when I think back to the Coca-Cola that Mrs. Usher gave me after having brought an unwanted juvenile delinquent to her home so he would not have to be locked in a cell on Thanksgiving. It was through stories like this that I learned who *I* really was. Despite my gruff exterior, my bad attitude, my lack of patience, and my short temper; inside me is a good person who has grown up to have a very kind and compassionate heart.

Today, *what* I am is an author, a child advocate, a faithful husband, a good father, and a loving grandfather. *Who* I am today is *me*, and that is all I ever wanted to be. My name is Roger, and I am glad to meet you.

Acknowledgments

I would like to acknowledge the many people who are or were, at one time, my friends. Each of them, in his or her own special way, brought something into my life. It might not have been something that these people actually did, but rather how they caused me to think, feel, or react in certain situations. Although, in some cases, some of my friends had a less-than-positive impact on my life, it was my reactions to those circumstances that helped me to become the person I am today. Dealing with irresponsible behavior showed me, in part, what type of person I really was. I saw that I was a friend who was always there for the people I cared for, no matter what, and that I was always willing to give more than I received.

To the following people I owe a very special thank you, not only for *what* I became but also for *who* I became: George Victor Usher, Rozie Eloise Usher, Robert "Bob" Sealander, Ann Conklin (Kaiser), Dian Williams (Kiser), Sharon Jackson, Judy Carter (Kiser), Lois Claxton (Moore), Garland Williams, Julie Stevens, Maggie Griest (Kaiser), Kevin Kaiser, Roger Kiser Jr.,

Chelsey Kiser, Madison Kiser, Karen (Kraus) Parks, Terry Persse, Danny Jones, Monty Shindler, Joseph Dabenigno, Raymond Ferranti, Craig Johnson, Dave Matthews, Lee Simonson, Nellie Huntley, Jim Hurley, Jimmy Williams, Maude Hunnicut, Wendell Leroy Archer, Joseph Wells, Dick Colon, Andrew Puel, Donald Watts, Joseph Wells, Wayne Evers, and Buela (Reed) Shiller.